D0868513

The Spirit in the Desert

Pilgrimages to Sacred Sites in the Owens Valley

Brad Karelius

We are pilgrims together.
Brad Karelius

Booksurge Charleston

ISBN: 1-4392-1721-1
ISBN-13: 9781439217214
LCCN: 2008910139

Visit www.booksurge.com to order additional copies.

Jesus said to them, 'Come away to a deserted place, all by yourselves and rest a while.'

MARK 6:31

What really matters is that I have taken the fundamental decision to begin the journey.

ALESSANDRO PRONZATO

Southern Pacific tracks through Owens Valley, c. 1940, Ansel Adams, Library of Congress.

To my wife, Janice,
and to our children, Kathryn and Erik,
for encouraging these journeys into sacred space.
And to Tom Hamilton, my lifelong friend and mentor

IN MEMORIAM

Jody Patterson (1941–2001)
matriarch of Swansea and Cerro Gordo

Dr. Loren Grey (1915–2007)
high school buddy of my father and son of Zane Grey

ACKNOWLEDGEMENTS

This book was written with a lot of help from Jack Graham. He organized my composition and created the maps to help you find the sites. Jack's passion for this project gave me hope and inspiration to follow through. Thanks also to Bill Wallace, who helped with the initial formatting of the text and photos.

Thank you to those who read the manuscript and offered important criticism and ideas: Dr. Walter Bruggemann, Columbia Theological Seminary; Dr. Garry Wills, Northwestern University; Luan Mendel, Mammoth, CA; Dr. Lorraine Blair, Randsburg, CA; Dr. Leigh Harris, UCLA; Michael Patterson, Cerro Gordo, CA; Laura Saari Pulido, Santa Ana, CA; Dr. Larry Budner, MD, Santa Ana, CA; Phyllis Tickle, Senior Fellow of Cathedral College at the National Cathedral, Washington DC; and Dr. Michael Delacourt, CSU, Sacramento.

I am grateful for my spiritual directors who have guided me through interior deserts: Sister Jeanne Fallon of the Sisters of Saint Joseph of Orange and the Center for Spiritual Development; Father Gordon Moreland s.j., of the House of Prayer, Roman Catholic Diocese of Orange.

Thank you to the U.S. Geological Survey in Menlo Park, California, for use of their maps, and especially to Christy Ryan with the Science Information and Library Service, for all her patience in explaining the various types of maps and how to download and knit them together for use in this book.

Thank you to Mary Daniel of the Bookstore at the Manzanar National Historic Site and to her staff, and to the research staff at the Eastern California Museum, Independence, for their assistance in reviewing this book.

Finally, thank you to Denis Clarke and Source Books. Denis is the copy editor of this book and he lovingly polished the rough work. Over the years we have shared a ministry to the poor and homeless in Santa Ana and I am blessed to have his participation in this project.

PERMISSIONS

CONTENTS

Preface

We have learned in recent time that 'testimony' is the best bearer of truth, testimony as first person witness that is rooted in concrete experience. Brad Karelius is a powerful witness! What makes him compelling is his capacity for artistic articulation that permits the rest of us to feel and touch and taste—albeit at second hand—his own remarkable religious sense of the wide open reaches of the desert. Helped along by his son Erik, Brad has learned to observe in patient ways the specificity and the beauty of the strange brooding world in front of him. Without either a romantic mysticism or an assertive theological bent, he shows us the ways in which the wilderness is a place where the God of Healing can bivouac. Readers will be called out by Brad...away from the busyness of the technological rat-race. But not only called out from, but called out to... to quiet peaceableness, to healing voices, and to an overwhelming presence. Here is the testimony of a priest who has suffered enough. He has found in the wilderness more than enough for sustenance. This book bids the reader into the geography of grace that he himself has entered.

Walter Brueggemann
Columbia Theological Seminary
March, 2008

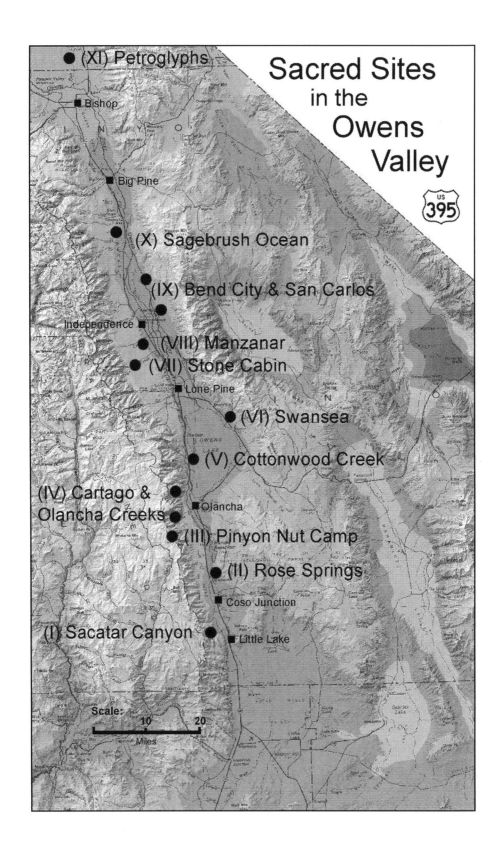

Sacred Sites in the Owens Valley

US 395

(XI) Petroglyphs

Bishop

Big Pine

(X) Sagebrush Ocean

(IX) Bend City & San Carlos

Independence

(VIII) Manzanar

(VII) Stone Cabin

Lone Pine

(VI) Swansea

(V) Cottonwood Creek

(IV) Cartago & Olancha Creeks

Olancha

(III) Pinyon Nut Camp

(II) Rose Springs

Coso Junction

(I) Sacatar Canyon

Little Lake

Scale:

10   20

Miles

JOIN ME IN THE DESERT

The desert, the mountain top, the frozen regions, the wild woods: all testify to the same experience of solitude and space. Spiritual maturity, like physical maturity, demands space, vastness, wildness.

Kenneth Leech

Deep into the night, an apple from the tree outside our bedroom falls upon the wooden deck. Jostled from sleep, our fourteen-year-old son, Erik, begins a strong seizure. I leap toward his bed, which is just four feet away from mine. On my knees I keep his head and flailing arms from hitting the wall. Erik's throat is seizing. He fights for air. I turn him on his side, speaking softly to him: "Everything is okay." Erik's seizures are routine for me and my wife, Jan. Every night between two and six o'clock, from deep sleep I startle into protective action.

Erik is fourteen and his six-foot frame is strong. The contractions can be violent and he can break a bone if he catches his arm in the bed railing. Every night, as I kneel at his bed, holding his trembling body and stroking his hair, I hurt for him.

The seizures usually last five minutes. Then I return to bed, lie on my back and stare up at the dark ceiling. "Are you okay?" I ask. "Fine. Okay," Erik responds. His breathing returns to normal. I watch carefully for a second seizure, which can launch into *status epilepticus* or a long series of seizures that can be broken only by a trip to the emergency room and Valium. Moonlight shines through the window onto Erik. I can see the rhythmic rise of his breathing. His face is now peaceful in sleep.

1

THE SPIRIT IN THE DESERT

My heart is still racing. Fear and anxiety pass through me. For times like this, everybody has a place in the imagination where they can find peace and serenity. For some it is the ocean, for others, the sound of rain. I reconnect with serenity after these night crises by visiting the desert and the Owens Valley in my mind. That is where my spirit can rest in God. I see Highway 395 and the first glimpse of the Sierra Nevada. I hear the sound of desert wind blowing the sand and the whirling of creosote and sagebrush branches. In dark nights of my soul, my heart goes out to the desertland to meet God again.

And where do *you* go when anxiety makes your heart race and fear seizes you?

I invite you to join me in the desert. I believe that when we experience God and the Spirit in a particular physical location, we can visit that place again later in our hearts. We can reconnect with the Presence that brings peace and thanksgiving.

I invite you to join me on a pilgrimage to sacred sites in the Owens Valley.

I am suddenly awake. It is time! The alarm clock beside the bed indicates five a.m. I hear the soft rhythmic snores of the family asleep. I am awakened by the excitement of beginning a journey.

Denim shirt, Wrangler jeans, belt, Justin boots. A weathered black Stetson is on the front seat of the car. Quietly I walk out into the early morning light. I am on the road. No good need for coffee; the adrenaline is pumping. I focus on the long journey ahead. I drive east on Highway 91 from Orange County towards Corona in light traffic, but heading west there is a ten-mile queue. The new Interstate 15 cutoff comes quickly and it is hard to see in the fog. Soon I sense the climb up through the Cajon Pass which leads to the high desert and Las Vegas.

As I maneuver past truck caravans through the soup, I think of Moses climbing cloud-shrouded Mount Sinai. I must concentrate. Finally, there is the familiar sign: Cajon Summit 4200 feet, marker to the Borderland, entrance to a place of luminous wonder.

Within minutes the clouds dissipate to reveal the new light of dawn. Purple and yellow fleck the horizon. As the road drops onto a plain the tension of the drive is released and I know what is ahead. With a sigh of relief I make the turn onto Highway 395 and leave the bulk of traffic rolling behind me on the Interstate to Las Vegas.

This is another world. Senses are alert. The violet-tinged dawn brightens to an orange glow. An incredible view spills out before me: one hundred-and-eighty degrees of high desert, marked by Joshua trees uplifted in prayer and the spicy scent of sagebrush. Vast space. My heart opens to peace and thanksgiving as I enter again into God's desert, my spiritual homeland. Another retreat has begun.

Of course, instant serenity is too much to expect. Work and cares do not lift like the fog. I have some hours of driving ahead in which to allow what I left behind to wander in and out of my thoughts: books, my studies, the people at the Church of the Messiah, my parish in Santa Ana, southern California, my checkered career—all that led me here.

"You are going *where?*" my colleague demanded.

My voice dropped. "I am going out to the desert for a retreat before Holy Week begins. I thought it would be a good idea."

"The desert!" The face was less than a foot away, eyes locked into mine. "The desert is where mass murderers go to dump bodies or to hide out from the police. Think of those godforsaken places with little, decrepit *Psycho* motels—when you least expect it, zap! you're dead! I wouldn't go to the desert for a retreat if it was the last place on earth!"

So much for putting new ideas out for peer review. Word got out at the parish, "Father Brad is going to the desert for a Lenten retreat." The Directress of the Altar Guild pulled me aside after Sunday Eucharist, "I hear that you are going on a retreat in the desert? Are you going *alone?*"

"Yes. I thought that would make for a good retreat. Otherwise it might be construed as a vacation."

"You need to go prepared. Take a gun." Her pastoral concern reminded me that her husband was a retired FBI agent.

But when I made my first retreat into the wilderness of Owens Valley, California, in March 1990, I bore no firearm nor met any mass murderers. And I discovered that with the Holy Spirit in the desert, anything could happen.

Since then, the rhythm that has developed for me is to make a desert retreat during Advent and Lent which for Christians are traditionally special periods of prayer, self-reflection and mindfulness of God. The experiences and graces emerging from these retreats have found expression in sermons and the spiritual direction I give to parishioners and other seekers of God. The rhythm of my desert retreats has become normative to Messiah Parish life. As Advent and Lent draw close, people now ask me with a different tone, "When are you going back to the desert?"

THE SPIRIT IN THE DESERT

The most wonderful grace of all has been that the parishioners who engage me at coffee hour and remark pensively, "You know, I think I want to go out to the desert too." Seeds of grace.

The Spirit in the desert also touched the desert fathers and mothers of the fourth century, the Celtic saints, and the medieval mystics. How wonderful that my desert encounters can connect with these other movements of the Spirit, so that Julian, Columba, Patrick, Teresa and Anthony are familiar friends! We have walked in the same land.

In his book, *Living Between Worlds: Place and Journey in Celtic Spirituality*, Philip Sheldrake has helped me to reflect on these years of desert journeys to see that Christians have long had a fascination for the desert or wilderness. I have been reminded how important the desert was to the fourth century monks of Syria, Palestine and Egypt.

> Christian monasticism…originated in the kingdom of the scorpion and the hyena; a world of rock and heat. Several centuries later the biographers of holy men in northwest Europe depicted their subjects as seekers after landscapes and environments which were correspondingly forbidding.

Sheldrake also shares that the Celtic ascetics, Columba and Cuthbert, sent others in search of the desert on the borderlands of the then settled world. For the Celtic monks, the ideal site for religious settlement offered both seclusion and accessibility.

> In the search for holiness and spiritual experience, there was a creative tension between the desire for seclusion and the wish to be accessible and open to the society at large. This expresses in a particular way a theological balance between transcendence and eminence in the Celtic experience of God.

The sacred sites which I have chosen for my walks with the Spirit, are close to amenities such as paved roads and small towns. They are also in vast, open, empty places, where there is silence and solitude.

Bishop Tom Shaw of the Episcopal Diocese of Massachusetts led the 1996 Spring Clergy Retreat for the Episcopal Diocese of Los Angeles. He spoke of the early desert fathers and mothers who had left the cities of Constantine's empire.

> The desert fathers and mothers were a spiritual reaction to the urban captivity of Christianity under Constantine. They went out into the desert to get away from all of this. In banks of the wadis or dry gulches they made their dugouts. In time, a dozen, up to a hundred of these hermits would come under the supervision of an abbot or abbess who would oversee what they had in common. One of the key responsibilities of the abbot was the direction of the Holy Week liturgies, and the custom arose for the abbot to go far out into the desert for solitude in preparation for this holy time. The desert would be cooler and greener at this time of year.

Bishop Shaw helped me make another connection. The Lenten retreat into the desert in March was when I prepared for the complex liturgies that we try to do well at Messiah Parish. Late spring is a time when the desert of Owens Valley is most hospitable to strangers. The months of November and early December for Advent retreat are also comfortable, before the cold winds and snow return.

I am still driving, but no longer at Interstate speed. I've been behind a rickety camper van all the way along the Pearblossom Highway—and happy with the pace. And I realize that, quiet, slow and alone, with no fancy liturgy in sight, I have actually been praying.

> When you pray, go into your room and shut the door and pray to your Father who is in secret, and your Father who sees in secret will reward you.
>
> Matthew 5:6

This is good, surely, the whole idea of Retreat. But I am not yet in a blissful state of continual prayer because suddenly the intellect kicks in and I find myself thinking of a passage in a book, *The Desert: An Anthology for Lent,* by John Moses which I took up in preparation for now. Moses quotes the well-known Trappist monk, Thomas Merton:

It is true that the solitary life must also be a life of prayer and meditation, if it is to be authentically Christian...But what prayer! What meditation!... Utter poverty. Often an incapacity to pray, to see, to hope...a bitter, arid struggle to press forward through a blinding sandstorm.

Do not mistake my meaning. It is not a question of intellectual doubt... It is something else, a kind of doubt that questions the very roots of a person's own existence, a doubt which undermines their very reason for existing and for doing what they do. It is this doubt which reduces a person finally to silence, and in the silence which ceases to ask questions, they receive the only certitude they know: The presence of God in the midst of uncertainty and nothingness, as the only reality but as a reality which cannot be placed or identified.

Do *I* have this uncertainty, this doubt, this incapacity to pray? If I do, who am I kidding, taking off to the desert to commune with Cuthbert and Columba? If I do *not,* would Merton call me an inauthentic Christian? Suddenly, my mind is reeling. Best to leave the questions aside for the moment. Deep breath! Concentrate on practical matters for now.

PRACTICAL MATTERS

It is the search for God—and God alone—which lies at the heart of the desert story.

John Moses

The hardest part of making a retreat is the beginning: is it really okay for me to do this, to take the time? I believe that it is particularly difficult for men to give themselves permission to make a retreat because our identities are bound up in a sense of duty to work—what business do we have going on retreat when we should be at work?

Religious communities have long seen how their clergy have benefited from time given to a retreat. They see it in positive behavior changes and a renewed focus to vocation. Clergy who take time for retreats bring their own spiritual renewal into their preaching and interactions with parishioners. Many new pastors now have in the initial letter of agreement with their congregations, time allotted to at least one annual retreat. Only when I had gone through the process of justifying the time to myself and had cleared everything with my family and parish, several months in advance, would I write 'Desert Retreat' in red ink in my Franklin Planner.

But why would the California desert be the place for a retreat? For many people it is not an especially inviting space: a monotony of miles of sand and sagebrush to dash through on the way to Las Vegas or the Colorado River. Friends have long tried to entice me to go to the Holy Land to see the real desert of the Bible. When they have responded to my own invitation to visit the California desert, they have been surprised to experience in Death Valley and the Owens Valley the same desert milieu as is vividly described in the Hebrew Scriptures.

I have grown up in Southern California, and the surrounding desert lands are familiar to me. They may be new to you. In this book I am focusing on the Owens Valley and Eastern Sierra, but I have also made retreats into Death Valley. These areas are within a four-hour drive from Los Angeles. The route to the Owens Valley I prefer is Highway 395, which runs up the spine of California on its eastern side—the most spectacular highway I have driven. There are two routes to Highway 395 from southern California: via Highway 14 through Mojave, if you start in Los Angeles; and, from Orange County and the Inland Empire, along Interstate 15 via the Cajon Pass.

But what I am looking for is away from the highway. For several months before each retreat I read books by other desert travelers, histories of early desert settlements and accounts of Native American culture in the region. In these I look for a place that gives me a sense of history, or perhaps unusual geology, and plan to center myself there for the period of the retreat. When I first began these desert retreats, my restlessness and difficulty with slowing down made me travel too far. I would make a number of day journeys, spending more time driving than walking and praying. I encourage you to research a specific area that interests you, minimize car travel after you arrive and spend your time walking, the better to appreciate the beauty and majesty that is often lost to speed. Seek out a place where you will have solitude and silence but which is not too far from a paved road. Find a place where you can walk into the wilderness, into the emptiness, feel the story and presence of the people who may have lived there, and let God work with you in that place. God will touch you in a wonderful way.

After I have identified an area of focus for the next retreat, I will get my hands on a topographic map of that area. I have found Allied Maps (alliedmaps.com) an excellent resource. They have the most extensive collection of 7.5-degree topographic maps and desert guides in California. The DeLorme map collections for Northern and Southern California are very useful too.

As you enter Owens Valley on Highway 395, its quiet energy and power can be intensely compelling. Sometimes there is an irony that accompanies you, for breathing down your neck, riding your bumper and flashing headlights are the hell-bent drivers of Jeeps, Explorers and Ford Expeditions headed to the ski slopes of Mammoth Mountain at eighty miles-an-hour. These driven folk who leave work early on a Friday and try to get to Mammoth with a minimum of breaks are the greatest hazard of your desert journey. Accidents along this road are more often due to people falling asleep at the wheel than to drunk drivers. They nod off for a few seconds, wake up as they drift off the highway, overcorrect, and end up rolling the vehicle.

Such are the nuts and bolts of finding a suitable place for retreat. Giving yourself to a retreat in this desert land will awaken a renewed sense of thanksgiving for life and appreciation for the people who surround you.

I am still driving into the Owens Valley, prepared with my advance reading and my maps, enjoying the gorgeous scenery, aware of the danger of lunatic drivers. And I begin composing a Sunday sermon in my head. Perhaps this is too much like work to be part of my retreat, perhaps not. But I do not fight it... *Running on Empty,* yes, that would be a good title.

A cold February morning. I am driving downhill through serpentine Rattlesnake Canyon, entering Death Valley. I almost miss the sign: No Gas Next 60 Miles. My sleepy eyes look at the gauge and a cold feeling of anxiety seizes me: almost empty. The last gas station is in Beatty, Nevada, 70 miles behind me. Will I make it? I take my foot off the gas and coast downhill. My breath is tightening. Out of gas in Death Valley!

One of America's most beautiful highways is 395, running north and south on the eastern edge of the Sierra Nevada. I am attentive, alert in this life-filled landscape. Then behind me, riding my tail...

I am amazed at how these people who press pedal to the metal can be oblivious to the spiritual power of this incredible place. What seems to be a wasteland, a huge pile of sand and rocks, a flat, dead lake, pulses with life and the presence of God. What appears to be nothingness is pregnant with potential: a rain shower will generate carpets of wildflowers. Come prepared to be awake and ready for surprises and the close, loving embrace of God. The lava flows, the crystal lakes, the golden leaves of cottonwood trees, the silver sand dunes—and always the possibility of surprise—are there for those who have eyes to see.

The driver who falls asleep at the wheel, the driver who is too bleary to monitor his fuel, can be metaphors for you and me: when we are not awake and aware of the presence of God, we fall asleep. We are responsible for the trouble we get into.

Our life with God in Jesus is one of balance. We run out of gas and fall asleep at the wheel when we are out of balance with God, with our own selves and with our neighbor.

As it happens, I later developed these thoughts and delivered them at the parish church during Advent of 2002. Nothing like driving in this beautiful land for making you reflective. I did not want to break the creative mood, but I was getting tired, and heeding my own warning, I pulled off the highway. I could just as well be reflective at rest. I cut the motor. In sudden quiet and solitude, a few hundred yards along a rutted track, I leaned back in my seat and found myself retracing the long, sometimes tortuous road that had brought me to this point.

THE JOURNEY BEFORE THE DESERT JOURNEYS

Behold, I am doing a new thing... for I give water in the wilderness, rivers in the desert, to give drink to my chosen people, the people whom I formed for myself that they might declare my praise.

Isaiah 43:18a, 20b-21

God's call is a voice sounding in the depths of our own dark, silent times. Four distinct periods in my life have been foundational in recognizing the voice of God and knowing God's all-embracing love.

1965, three months before the Watts Riot, three in the morning. I was lying on my bed in my little apartment on the edge of Watts, South Central Los Angeles. My personal life was a mess. I was twenty years old, a pre-med student at the University of Southern California. My dream was to become a pediatrician. But I was beginning to discover a dark side to myself. I had become a compulsive liar, creating stories about my life that were not true and probably fed by a lack of self-esteem. I had accomplished a lot in my high school days, but college life was lonely, especially after the break-up of a three-year relationship with someone who rightly could not tolerate my pathology. I blamed my parents for the troubles in my life and did not see them for almost a year,

11

even though they lived just fifteen miles away in Pasadena. My science grades were dropping, and the vision of medical school was flying out the window.

I remember the stone-cold awareness creeping over me as I gazed up at the darkness in my apartment. An inner voice spoke: *So this is what it is like to grow up, to experience this awful, lonely, gnawing pain and sadness.* I was deeply depressed and I can now see how vulnerable I was then to substance abuse, acts of anger and aggression and self-destruction. Yet within the darkness of that night I experienced a Presence. What was this? It was not coming from thinking or contemplating. It was a deeply felt sense of something outside myself that was communicating a wondrous hope: I was *loved* and all would be well. I remembered the ending of Psalm 139:

Search me, O God, and know my heart:
Test me and know my anxious thoughts.
See if there be any offensive way in me,
And lead me in the way everlasting.

I slept soundly the rest of that night and woke up to the light of a new day. The hollow, hopeless feeling that had eaten at my stomach like an ulcer for many weeks was no longer there. I felt hungry again. And I needed to go back to church. I had not been to my home parish for many months.

On this new day, Sunday, the first day of God's creation of the world, I set out for St. Mark's Episcopal Church in Altadena, a two-hour journey by bus and foot. As soon as I entered the church, and knelt at the pew, I had a sense of homecoming. I was not alone. Familiar faces nodded greetings. The priest welcomed me with a bear hug. I cried through the whole liturgy and could hardly swallow the communion bread and wine. I was loved and all would be well.

At choir practice that Thursday night I joined a small community of other students and adults who were having a lot of fun practicing the hymns for the coming Sunday. Within a month I was teaching a wild bunch of third-graders in the Sunday School, frequently chasing after boys who escaped out the back window.

I had found a community that loved and encouraged me, where I could be myself, and where there were no dumb questions. The priests modeled the open-minded spirit that is so important in the Episcopal Church. And then the seeds of a call to ordination were planted in me when the Rector returned from Selma, Alabama, to tell about his experience in the great march with Dr. Martin Luther King, Jr.

June 1966, Braunschweig, West Germany. I had changed my major to history and German, trading the dream of a life in medicine for the vocation of college professor. I continued to struggle with depression. That I had rediscovered religious faith did not fix my life, although some skilled pastoral counseling had helped me to live in the real world. It was years before I would discover the consequences of growing up as a child of an alcoholic. As most addicted persons will testify, I had within me a deceptive voice that kept convincing me to make destructive decisions.

That same month, (on my twenty-first birthday,) I had been arrested for trying to sell to a bookstore in Pasadena some historic books that I had stolen from the Doheny Library at USC. It must have broken the hearts of my parents when the Pasadena Police called them to pick me up. I was preparing to leave for Germany, for a summer job at Heimbs Kaffee, in Braunschwieg, which was owned by friends of a friend. It was an opportunity to build my language skills. The university decided not to press charges and allowed me to make the trip. Judgment Day would come in September, when I returned.

I worked very hard at the coffee factory during those three months in Germany. I rarely encountered anyone who spoke English. I lived at the YMCA in the center of a medieval city that had been all but destroyed in an American-British bombing raid in 1944. Across the street was the scorched stone façade of the Jewish synagogue burned on Krystallnacht. Looking back, if ever there was a situation which fostered depression, this would be it it: cultural and physical isolation and the ever-present sense of guilt and foreboding that something terrible was going to happen when I returned to USC in September.

Almost every day I visited Saint Andreas Lutheran Church, a huge, twelfth-century gothic edifice one block away from the YMCA. I always found an open door. Entering the restored building I would be filled with the scent of recently poured concrete. The interior was now very plain as the magnificent Rococo interior had been destroyed in the bombing of 1944. I never saw anyone in the church except on Sundays. I would walk to the altar and sit for a long time in the pastor's chair. I had a lot for which to feel guilty and terrible, but the Presence visited me again and again: *I am loved and all will be well.* I trusted this voice.

I returned to Los Angeles in September. At a meeting with the Dean of Students, I was told: "Mr. Karelius, you are a thief and we do not need you at USC." I know that once again I had wounded my parents, but it was justice.

A week later, my Uncle John Trever helped me to enroll at Baldwin-Wallace College, Berea, Ohio, where he was a professor of religious studies. Uncle John was the first person to identify the Dead Sea Scrolls as authentic, when he was in Jerusalem in 1946. He was a great teacher of the Bible, brought me under his wing and guided me through this opportunity to finish college. In that one year in Berea, the world of the dramatic arts opened up to me. I wrote and produced a play, and found a creative outlet for my imagination.

During that year, too, I felt a strengthening call to vocation in the Church. The Diocese of Los Angeles would not sponsor me for seminary because of my misdeeds at USC, but Uncle John, a Methodist, encouraged me to go off to seminary at the ecumenical Pacific School of Religion, in Berkeley, where I could pursue the study of religion and explore ordination.

Berkeley, 1967–1970, was the center of America's cultural revolution. During these years that I attended seminary I found it to be already inclusive of women, gays and lesbians, and persons of color. I was to be well prepared for my future in the Episcopal Church. God has a sense of humor and forgiveness, and I was ordained a priest on December 15, 1971.

June 16, 1987. The third foundational encounter with the presence of God came as terrifying surprise. It was during a flight from Los Angeles to Boston. My wife Jan, daughter Katie, son Erik, and I were on our way to our usual month-long vacation with Jan's family near Boston. In the middle of the flight, four-year-old Erik went into *status epilepticus*–a continuous seizure. He had encephalitis. It was an unexpected reactivation of a disease Erik briefly had when he was ten days old. Our month's vacation was spent at Massachusetts General Hospital in Boston. Erik came out of the hospital alive, but with severe frontal lobe damage. He was to become an eternal four-year-old. Erik's life is now very precariously balanced with medication. He has daily seizures, and when the drug levels are out of whack he cannot walk and vomits his guts out. We call the paramedics when we cannot stop the seizures. In the last thirty months he has been in hospital three times, his life under threat. Through these years we have learned to live one day at a time. Good days are precious. Bad days can flare up in an instant.

How could Jan and I get through these times and not be terrified by fear of the future, without again remembering the presence of Jesus, and having eyes open enough to receive grace when God sends it to us?

The fourth foundational event has been the most serious call that God has given to me—more serious than the call to priesthood. The call to contemplative prayer has been a true grace, as God pours love upon us in abundance. By 1989 I was rector of the Church of the Messiah, a growing urban parish, in Santa Ana, California. The congregation had changed significantly in eight years: from a small parish of older Anglos, into an ethnically, economically and culturally diverse congregation of Latinos, African-Americans, long-time Anglo members, and a growing gay-lesbian membership. The parish had developed several important outreach ministries. The staff had grown to include four clergy. The pledge base had increased from $49,000 to $300,000.

Out of the blue, I was drawn into the search process for a new rector at All Saints Episcopal Church in Beverly Hills. I went along with the initial series of interviews, not quite believing that I could be a serious candidate. After all, the congregation was full of Hollywood stars; Fred Astaire was an usher at the morning Eucharist. Beverly Hills was not Santa Ana.

In June 1989, Jan and I made a three-day visit to the parish. I was on a short-list of three for the position. Heady stuff! It took my breath away. It was hard to be centered and not distracted by the allure of the place.

The final interview consisted of the vestry quizzing me at length on each of the following subjects: Christian education, liturgy, music, outreach, stewardship, and administration. No problems! But then came a final question. It was about spirituality. The congregation at All Saints enjoyed a long history of prayer groups and various spiritual disciplines. That day I discovered that my own spiritual life was a blank page.

I could talk about reading Morning Prayer, I could talk about Saint Teresa, I could describe the foundational experiences of God in my past life. But at that particular juncture, my conversation with God that had begun as a cry in the darkness, and had continued in an old German church, and then as desperate pleading in a pediatric intensive care unit —was not a daily, fostered relationship of prayer. I thank God for that moment of revelation and that I was not called to be rector to the stars. I believe that position would have become a distraction from God's dream for me.

I had to do something about my spiritual deficiency. God led me to the Center for Spiritual Development, in Orange, California, an ecumenical resource for prayer and spiritual disciplines, sponsored by the Sisters of Saint Joseph of Orange. I met Sister Jeanne Fallon, who had become a spiritual director at the Center after twenty years of mission work in Papua New Guinea. In our first few months, Sister Jeanne guided me through various classical forms of prayer. I had been a priest for twenty years, but I felt like a novice. I met her each month to share what was happening between Jesus and me. She was not so much a director as a coach, helping me to find firm footholds, reminding me that God is loving and close, and that there is no 'perfected style of prayer,' and that I must keep my eyes on Jesus.

A new group was forming for the Nineteenth Annotation of the Spiritual Exercises of Saint Ignatius. This five-hundred-year-old curriculum of daily scripture readings and long periods of silent meditation had been modernized. I began the program with Sister Jeanne, and we met weekly for twelve months to share and reflect.

The beginnings of the Exercises reminded me of starting up at a health club. I remember the first week. In the evening after dinner, I went to Erik's old room. I sat on the floor, legs crossed, with my back supported by the bed. I opened my Bible to the brief scripture reading for that day which I would read aloud. Then I would meditate in silence for ten minutes. I used to set a timer so that I would know when the time was up. The first two minutes were okay. Then the brain started grinding into gear: I thought about the tasks of the next day, argued with people with whom I had issues, went into the past to remember hurtful events. To the past and the future my mind skipped —anywhere but the present. Ten minutes were an hour.

After the meditation I would wash dishes or do some other chore. Then I would write in my journal about what I had noticed was going on within me, for example, the difficulty with staying in the present. I listened for those moments when I sensed peace, love, hope and joy. Later, I would be able to collect those experiences together under the name Consolation. I also listened for those moments when the inner critic or judge began to speak. I noticed associated feelings of hurt, anger, guilt, and confusion. These I would be able to name Desolation.

I learned from Sister Jeanne some other key parts of meditation such as intentional breathing, correct posture and how to keep that inner critic from taking over my thoughts. Eventually, the ten minutes became forty-five.

The scriptures used by Saint Ignatius move through the fundamental experiences of God's love, and our sin and redemption in the life and ministry of Jesus, including the events of Holy Week and the Resurrection. Using these scriptures as focal points, I practiced different styles of contemplative prayer and developed a version that worked for me. The long periods of contemplative prayer became a vital part of my daily life. The present moment became more present.

At some point, people noticed changes in me: my presence with them, the spirit of my preaching and presiding at Eucharist. I had been a priest for twenty years and, as Marcus Borg expresses it, I "seemed to be meeting Jesus again for the first time." Words in the Psalms became my lament and my thanksgiving. Scripture passages seemed to be uttered in the present tense, as if the Word had been written especially for me to hear and speak. I could now put a face on the Presence that I had been sensing over the past thirty years: Jesus. This Presence was palpable. My conversations with Jesus, my review of the events in each day as I lay on my bed before sleep, became an interwoven communion and connection, became prayer. "Prayer is a conscious relationship with God", writes William Barry s.j. I have now come to recognize that prayer is as vital to my being as breathing.

But I was unprepared for the consequences of intimacy with God.

We do not remain the same person when we come into the presence of the Holy One. We cannot invite Jesus into intimate friendship and simply turn away from the shadow presence of our false self. As I grew closer to Jesus, the Holy Spirit brought to the fore those habits and practices that I was pretending were not really part of me. This was the false self I had patched together in my life up to this point.

I realized in cold shuddering truth, that I was not being honest with my wife, Jan, about our family finances. In the midst of hospital bills and inadequate income, I was spending more money than was coming in. I was using credit cards to buy things for the family and for the church. I would buy dinners, Christmas gifts, and pay for medication with the credit card, when I had no money in my checking account. I would buy lunch for a group of parishioners, put up homeless families in motels and pay for medical prescriptions, when I did not have the money. I wanted to be generous and to express appreciation and to help people in need. The credit cards were out of control.

Buying on credit was one of my addictions and a great secret that I kept from Jan. Prayer and the Spirit were compelling me to be honest with Jan about our financial problems.

When I did come clean with Jan and myself, I was led to certain Twelve Step programs, such as Adult Children of Alcoholics. There I met people who were trying to fill the void of emotional abandonment with similar addictions. I learned that if I listened to the deceptive voice within, I would hear all manner of clever, reasonable ways to rationalize more addictive behavior. Only by recognizing that my life was unmanageable and by allowing the power of God to heal and restore, could I be whole, and move toward Jesus as a disciple.

In sharing these inner desert experiences with you and these foundational encounters with God, I hope that I have communicated my belief that life with God and our journey toward holiness are not along a straight path. And the more God calls us into friendship and communion, the more we will be drawn into honesty under scrutiny of the Light. Each of us will have revealed to us a difficult path to follow.

These desert journeys, then, are the natural progression of God's call to me and my hunger to be in the presence of God. For meditation and prayer I go into Erik's room. The power of the desert also invites me into a different experience of the same redeeming love.

Exactly what is so fulfilling about the journeys in nature and the solitude and silence? In his book, *Who Do You Say I Am?*, William Barry shares a statement by British psychiatrist J. S. Mackenzie:

> The enjoyment of God should be the supreme end of spiritual technique; and it is in that enjoyment of God that we feel not only saved in the Evangelical sense, but safe; we are conscious of belonging to God, and hence are never alone; and, to the degree we have these two, hostile feelings disappear....In that relationship Nature seems friendly and homely; even its vast spaces instead of eliciting a sense of terror speak of the infinite love; and the nearer beauty becomes the garment with which the Almighty clothes Himself.

Grounded in these four foundational experiences of the love of God, friendship with Jesus, and compelling invitation of the Spirit, I come joyfully into this desert land. I walk for miles in endless sand, among gold shimmering aspen, yellow crowned cottonwoods, and with the caress of warm, dry winds. I lose all sense of time and naturally lift my hands in prayer and adoration, feeling to my very bones that I am loved and precious to God. In this land without fences and people, with the sound of rushing creeks, rustling wind in trees, and the dashing force of jackrabbits and deer, God's holy presence electrifies me.

When I return to ministry and the tasks that frequently cause me to forget God, in frantic moments and weight of exhaustion, I close my eyes, see that desert place again, and remember to Whom I belong, Who loves me without limit, and that I am not alone.

THE DUKE OF ORANGE COUNTY

John Wayne is the most obvious recent embodiment of that American Adam—untrammeled, unspoiled, free to roam, breathing in a larger air than the cramped men behind desks. *

Garry Wills

Corona del Mar, California, 1971. The blue Ford Galaxy station wagon has been following me for the last five minutes. From my rear-view mirror I read the bumper sticker on the front of the car: something about guns and the Viet Nam War. I am in Republican territory.

I turn into Fashion Island Mall and park. The blue car parks opposite and I can clearly see the driver. Oh, my God! John Wayne! The Duke! Living in Orange County, a priest in the resort town of Laguna Beach, I am not too surprised to run into celebrities. But *John Wayne!* I try to be cool in locking my car and walking over to J.C. Penny's. The Hollywood icon and his wife Pilar are right behind me. I hold the door for them. "Thanks, Padre," he murmurs. The Quiet Man himself.

We go our own ways in the huge store and I search for a nightgown for my wife. The cashier is wrapping my purchase when I am startled to see the Duke and his wife standing right next to me. The Duke is holding several nightgowns. They are regular customers, I find out. We make casual conversation. *I am talking with the Duke!*

* Reprinted with the permission of Simon & Schuster,Inc. from JOHN WAYNE'S AMERICA by Gary Wills. Copyright © 1997 by Literary Research Inc. All rights reserved.

I remember that I had been a roommate of his nephew at* USC. His father was Wayne's partner in Batjak Films. That gives us more to talk about. Then I remember that my Uncle Kenny played freshman football at USC at the time of the Duke. And so the conversation develops. Our business negotiations with J.C. Penny are complete and Pilar carries their purchases to the blue station wagon. But the Duke is not going anywhere. Somehow we are walking in the courtyard on the west side of the department store. Our common ground and the fact that I am a priest draw Wayne into personal sharing and conversation. The talk is very natural, as if we were old friends meeting after a long interval. As we walk, more connections between us transpire. The wedding of Barry Goldwater Junior, is coming up at my church, Saint Mary's, and John Wayne has been invited.

For a few minutes I am part of John Wayne's life. (I am convinced that given enough time we can find connections between ourselves and anyone). It seems as though he wants me to keep talking with him, but I am growing self-conscious. Though my pastoral intuition tells me that here is someone going through troubles and needs to talk, our conversation ends with me mumbling something about an appointment.

Only later did I discover the turmoil within John Wayne. That time we were walking about Fashion Island, finding connections with one another, the Duke's life was in distress. He was at the peak of his career, but there was terrific tension between the demands of his films and his family life. He wanted to take the family on location with him during the shoots which would mean three or four months away from home. Pilar felt that this was no way to raise their young children. Within twelve months of our conversation, Pilar and John would separate. In his book, *John Wayne's America: The Politics of Celebrity,* Garry Wills considers this separation to have been more generally significant:

> By a confluence of audience demand and commercial production, the Wayne that took shape in the transaction between the two expressed deep needs and aspirations that took 'Wayne' as the pattern of manly American virtue.

When you join this journey to the sacred sites of the Eastern Sierra and the Owens Valley, you will find yourself in John Wayne country in more ways than one.

As you drive north on Highway 395, you will see at the edge of the town of Lone Pine a twenty-foot billboard. It is empty now but for many years there was a colorful poster of a strong, silent cowboy advertising Marlboro cigarettes. The advertisement was the quintessential icon of this desert town until the 1999 agreement between cigarette makers and forty-six states required the removal of thousands of billboards, and now my favorite is gone.

When I make a retreat to the sacred desert sites I always stay at the Dow Villa Motel in the heart of Lone Pine. There is a historic plaque in front of the motel which tells of the making of the first western movies in the Alabama Hills, a few minutes north of town. You will read that John Wayne made his first western movies in Lone Pine and that his last appearance was in an advertisement for Great Western Savings Bank. The Duke used to stay at Dow Villa in room 20. When I stay in room 20, I imagine his presence there.

What is it about John Wayne that is so attractive? Garry Wills writes, "John Wayne defies the law of optics. The further away he is, the larger he becomes." There is no doubt that Wayne lived the character he portrayed. What is it that makes him the great western American? Certainly John Wayne personifies the folklore of the Cowboy West that, especially through movies, is known across the globe: the songs, the hats, the spurs, the self-contained law of the quick-draw—all the excitement of pressing into new land. It is a folklore that opens vistas for everyone. The hero of the folklore is the cowboy who, though historically lasting no more than a couple of generations, gave rise to more prose and poetry than any other hero in the human story. Perhaps the Japanese samurai come close, perhaps the Viking raider might if all his stories had been preserved.

Each year thousands of Europeans visit the Owens Valley and Lone Pine. A typical itinerary runs from San Francisco, down the Central Valley through Yosemite and Tioga Pass, south on Highway 395 to Lone Pine. From Lone Pine the Europeans head to Death Valley (even in the summer) and then on to Las Vegas. Often I have heard more German and French being spoken on the streets of Lone Pine than English. Europeans are fascinated with the wide-open spaces, and the mystique of the old west that permeates Lone Pine. And movie companies continue to film in the Alabama Hills; the films 'Maverick', 'Gladiator', 'Star Trek' and 'Iron Man,' are some of the recent productions.

In Wills' *John Wayne's America,* the Duke is presented as

the embodiment of American values [who] influenced our culture to a degree unmatched by any other public figure of his time.

(Certainly, John Wayne captures the essence of De Tocqueville's famous observations from a century before about America's unique rugged individualism). What does the image of John Wayne bring to your mind? Wills continues:

The West can deal with the largest themes in American history–beginning with the "original sins" of our country... It explores the relationship of people with the lands, of the individual with the community, of vigilante law to settled courts. With their themes of sacrifice, order and duty, Wayne's films were perfectly attuned to a new imperial America.

As we enter this desert land, birthplace of the western film genre, we also come to sacred sites, where people have sought communion with the Holy for thousands of years. What does it mean for a man, raised in a culture of John Wayne and rugged individualism, to seek communion with God?

Shortly before his death, in an interview with Barbara Walters, John Wayne revealed his own search:

I've always had deep faith that there is a Supreme Being, there has to be. To me that's just a normal thing to have this kind of faith. The fact that He has let me stick around a little longer certainly goes great with me–and I want to hang around as long as I'm healthy and not in anybody's way.

In most established cultures around the world, especially those of the East, the norm is for males to spend significant time and effort seeking God. Having gone through life's stages as students, workers, family men—after the birth of the first grandchild, a new chapter opens in their lives. The tradition is to leave the family and go off to the forest, an ashram, or a monastery. This is not a time to 'retire' in the Western sense; this is a time to attend to the most important focus of life–communion with God.

My sermons are inspired by this desert communion with God. (I include examples of two of these sermons, at the beginning and the end of this book). More and more men come up to me after a 'desert sermon', expressing, "I want to do that! I want to make the journey too." That is why I have written this book: to invite you, men and women, to seek communion with God in this vast and exhilarating expanse.

I remind myself that I am not writing a travelogue or a collection of romantic 'peak experiences.' I come into this land, to distance myself from the frantic busyness, the chorus of voices compelling me to this project, and that project. I come to place myself under the hot, direct rays of God's scrutiny and the loving embrace of Jesus that will never let me go. In the desert of God's love and scrutiny, John Wayne and the Marlboro man meet John the Baptist and Elijah.

Gail Sheehy has written a book entitled, *Understanding Men's Passages: Discovering the New Map of Men's Lives.* Sheehy's advice, based on demographic research, group interviews, medical commentary and personal testimony, is honest wisdom. Her most radical idea is that the first half of life, First Adulthood, is about

> ...crafting a 'false self'–a front tailored to please or to pass–that is useful in earning approval, rewards and recognition from the adult world.

But Second Adulthood, between the ages of about forty to seventy, is a whole new ball game. It is a time when

> ...there are a number of different scoreboards—as son, mate, father, friend, colleague, mentor, community wise man, benefactor. The crucial innings of Second Adulthood are neither played by the same rules nor scored in the same way as a young man's game. Men can succeed in second Adulthood, even reach an Age of Mastery, only if they move 'from competing to connecting' and aim for redirection rather than retirement.

The desert calls you and me to connection and communion with God in Jesus. From that foundational relationship, the Spirit gives us energy and wisdom for service and testimony. All the great mystics talk honestly about waking up to recognize their false self, and then, through personal encounters with God, seeing their true self in the life and ministry of Jesus.

THE SPIRIT IN THE DESERT

The American icons of John Wayne and the Marlboro Man celebrate rugged individualism. Louis L'Amour incarnates these images in his wonderful western novels, expressing the frontier virtues of hard work, perseverance, tenacity, and skill in outdoor survival. But the desert has its own way, with sand, wind and time, grinding gigantic boulders into grains of sand. The facade of stoic self-reliance soon blisters and wilts in the blasting heat and relentless, dry wind. The stories of western wanderers in the desert, on the edge of death by thirst or hunger, are enveloped in the dust storm. Emerging out of the cloud are the larger Biblical figures, shaped by Exodus into unconditional faith in the power of God to be what God wills to be.

Zane Grey's *Wanderer of the Wasteland* tells of a western man's harrowing journey into the arid southwestern deserts. His guilt and sin drive him toward a cruel and violent place that inspires his ultimate fate...Death Valley. The hero, Wansfell, meets an old prospector, Dismukes, full of desert wisdom, who reveals:

> "I was talkin' about what men think the desert means to them. In my case I say gold, an' I say that as the other man will claim he loves the silence or the color of the loneliness. But I'm wrong, an' so is he. The great reason why the desert holds men lies deeper. I feel that. But I've never had the brains to solve it. I do know, however, that life on this wasteland is fierce an' terrible. Plants, reptiles, beast, birds, an' men all have to fight for life far out of proportion to what's necessary in fertile parts of the earth. You will learn that early, an' if you are a watcher an' a thinker you will understand it.

> "The desert is no place for white men. An oasis is fit for Indians. They survive there. But they don't thrive. I respect the Indians. It will be well for you to live a while with Indians. Now what I most want you to know is this."

> The speaker's pause this time was impressive, and he raised one of his huge hands, like a monstrous claw, making a gesture at once eloquent and strong.

> "When the desert claims men it makes most of them beasts. They sink to that fierce level in order to live. They are trained by the eternal strife that surrounds them. A man of evil nature survivin' in the desert becomes more terrible than a beast. He is a vulture. On the other hand, there are

men whom the desert makes like it. Yes–fierce an' elemental an' terrible, like the heat an' the storm an' the avalanche, but greater in another sense– greater though that eternal strife to live–beyond any words of mine to tell. What such men have lived–the patience, the endurance, the toil–the fights with men an' all that makes the desert–the wanderin's an' perils an' tortures–the horrible loneliness that must be fought hardest, by mind as well as action–all these struggles are beyond ordinary comprehension an' belief. But I know. I've met a few such men, an' if it's possible for the divinity of God to walk abroad on earth in the shape of mankind, it was invested in them. The reason must be that in the development by the desert, in case of these few men who did not retro grade, the spiritual kept pace with the physical. It means these men never forgot, never reverted to mere unthinking instinct, never let the hard, fierce, brutal action of survival on the desert kill their souls. Spirit was stronger than body. I've learned this of these men, though I never had the power to attain it. It takes brains. I was only fairly educated. An' though I've studied all my years on the desert, an' never gave up, I wasn't big enough to climb as high as I can see. I tell you all this, Wansfell, because it may be your salvation. Never give up to the desert or to any of its minions! Never cease to fight! You must fight to live–an' so make that fight equally for your mind an' your soul. Thus you will repent for your crime, whatever that was. Remember–the secret is never to forget your hold on the past– your memories–an' through thinkin' of them to save your mind an' apply it to all that faces you out there."

Rising from his seat, Dismukes made a wide, sweeping gesture, symbolical of a limitless expanse. "An' the gist of all this talk of mine–this hope of mine to do for you as I'd have been done by–is that if you fight an' think together like a man meanin' to repent of his sin–somewhere out there in the loneliness an' silence you will find God!"

I am thinking of the enormous passion that drives men and women across emigrant trails for days without water, and the stirring within our own hearts when we read about valiant heroism in military battle. How can I, as an American male, shaped and influenced by John Wayne and the other film cowboys and heroes, be a spiritual warrior for God? How can I find that deep passionate place within me, discern the 'God-shaped void which only God can fill,' and bring that energy and hunger into my desert search for communion with God?

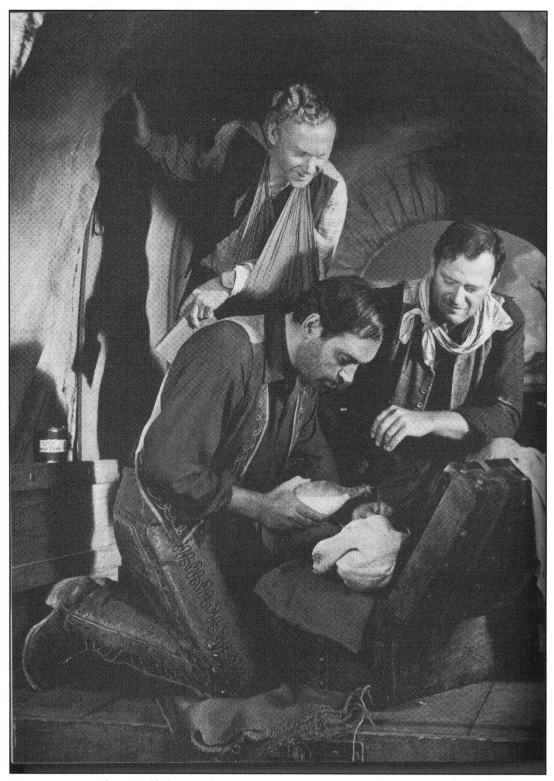

Baptism scene, 'Three Godfathers' with Harry Carey Jr., Pedro Armendariz, John Wayne. 1948, filmed in Lone Pine.

BRAD KARELIUS

You can walk in the footsteps of John Wayne and other Western film icons when you visit the Beverly and Jim Rogers Museum of Lone Pine Film History, located on Highway 395 at the south end of town. Its mission is to celebrate and preserve the movie history of Lone Pine, Death Valley and the Eastern Sierra areas. It also explores the interpretive and artistic expression of the western landscape. In addition to displays of artifacts for many movies filmed in the area, a state-of-the-art theater presents a history of films made in Lone Pine. www.lonepinefilmhistorymuseum.org

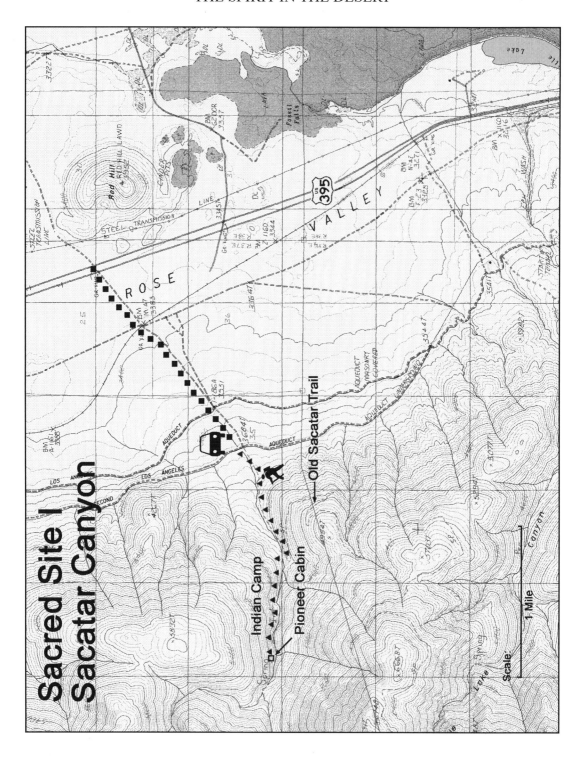

SACRED SITE I
SACATAR CANYON

Be sober, be watchful. Your adversary the devil prowls around like a roaring lion, seeking someone to devour. Resist him, firm in your faith.

I Peter 5:8-9a

This is a journey to a Sierra canyon west of Highway 395. It is the site of a typical Owens Valley Paiute settlement.

Drive north on Highway 395, passing through Little Lake, and you will soon come to an important natural formation, Red Cinder Cone (local name for Red Hill). The highway is divided at this point. After Red Cinder Cone, a dirt road will leave the highway heading west toward the Sierra Nevada. If you miss it, you can easily turn around further up the road and find the turn-off when you are southbound.

A good dirt road will lead you towards the small canyon ahead of you in the Sierra foothills. You are driving through open cattle range, so keep a careful eye out for little calves. Use care not to get between a calf and its mother.

As you drive west, you will come to a long line of poured concrete. This is the covering of part of the second Los Angeles Aqueduct. Turn your car around and park,

31

so that you are not blocking the road. The road to Sacatar Canyon is too rough for most cars to negotiate from this point.

Begin your hike to the canyon. You will slowly gain elevation, so take your time. And, since this is our first trip on foot, a warning to be sure to hike safely: take enough water, let someone know where you are going and when you plan to be back, and make sure your hat is on your head and your boots in good repair.

As you hike towards the canyon, notice how the desert ecology changes due to elevation. The streambed is dry and there seems to be no sign of life. You will pass a few huge boulders. Paiute Indians would sit on top of these boulders to sight game and to chip arrowheads. You may see some obsidian chips at the base of the boulders. Gilreath, a scholar of the Berkeley Archaeological Research facility, gives us some background:

> The Owens Valley Paiute 'tribes' were mobile clans, which moved about, depending on the season of the year. Within each of the Sierra canyons a Paiute clan staked out territory to which it returned at regular intervals. As native populations grew in the valley, semi-permanent lowland villages emerged, resulting in more intensive use of resources within smaller foraging areas. With the development of inherited chieftainship, territory was more rigorously defended.

At the mouth of Sacatar Canyon, you will see the old Sacatar Trail climbing to your left; it eventually crosses to Kennedy Meadows and over the Sierra. This was a major Native American route which was used for thousands of years. On entering Sacatar Canyon, there is a trail on the left side of the streambed and another that walks the right side. Take the path on the right.

As you climb, look back occasionally and note your elevation. Red Cinder Cone becomes more distant. In the mountains east of Red Cinder Cone is an obsidian deposit, which, for Native Americans, was an important source of this useful material (as we see later also at Rose Spring). In the Coso Mountains, further to the east are ancient hot springs, where Native American ceremonies were held and shamans prepared for their vision quests. In these mountains are some of the finest and best-preserved petroglyphs in North America. The area in which they can be seen is used for naval weapons testing, so entry is very limited and by permit only. Contact the Maturango Museum for their schedule of petroglyph tours.

There is soon a turn in the canyon wall and vegetation becomes more lush. This riparian area contains cottonwood, wild grape, willow and canyon phacelia–an annual lavender flower. (Cf. Wuerthner, p.62) If you listen carefully, you will hear the sound of running water. Then, all of a sudden, there is the water from the Sierra snowmelt. In the fall the trees are shimmering gold. In the spring, new green shoots of life are bursting forth. As the trail gradually climbs higher, you will see why we are on the right side of the canyon: emerging from the riverbed is a very dense blackberry patch, which would be hard to get through from the path on the left side.

On the right or north side of the canyon, evidence of Native American settlement becomes pronounced. Chips from arrowhead-making are all over the place. You will see old fire rings and some larger stone circles where shelters once stood.

The canyon narrows and the hike becomes challenging. I would stop here. At this point you will have another surprise. On the edge of the stream bed, in the shelter of cottonwoods and aspen, are the ruins of a pioneer cabin.

Ellen Cooper remembers growing up in this area in the 1920's:

That winter we arrived in Rose Valley in our covered wagon along with a small burro wagon, and leading our Jersey milk cow behind. We never got into the mountains that first winter, but spent it in the valley at the Sam Lewis Pack Station. I still remember when our mother would hitch up our mare named Babe to a buggy and go down the valley to Little Lake for the mail and groceries. It wasn't until the next spring we moved up to the homestead in Long Canyon. The winter of 1920, we lived in a tent.

All of our staples were ordered in bulk form from Los Angeles, and came up on the railroad. Once each month my father William would saddle his pack-string and travel eighteen miles down to the depot. He had a little tin shack in the mouth of Sacatar Canyon where he would spend the night and travel back up the long mountain trail the next day. Among the staples we bought were flour, sugar, lard, coffee, oatmeal, and peanut butter in ten-pound buckets. All our vegetables were grown in our large garden, and there was plenty of meat in the mountains."

This was a good place for the Native Americans to live in the desert. There are water, berries, and lots of game. It looks like a deer freeway here, with all the droppings.

Red Cinder Cone (Red Hill), near Little Lake, 2007. Author's photograph.

One autumn afternoon I sat on a boulder near the old cabin. The flat, brush area of the old Indian encampment surrounded me. I could imagine the large clan gathered, going through daily routines.

They had a strong sense of what went into the stewardship of this place. The resources were to be used carefully. Water and game and berries were not consumed with a sense of entitlement, the relationship to the resources was one of harmony. While they might defend the village site from other clans, the Indians did not have a sense of private property. All living things co-existed with them. Prayers were offered in apology and thanksgiving to the deer, before they hunted. While daily life was a struggle, they sensed a powerful spirit-force binding all things, animate and inanimate, into a cosmic kinship.

Here is a poem by John Lame Deer from the book *Meditations with Native Americans–Lakota Spirituality,* edited by P. Steinmetz.

I'm an Indian.
I think about common things like this pot.
The bubbling water comes from the rain cloud.
It represents the sky.
The fire comes from the sun
Which warms us all, men, animals, trees.
The meat stands for the four-legged creatures,
Our animal brothers,
Who gave of themselves so that we should live.
The steam is living breath.
It was water, now it goes up to the sky,
Becomes a cloud again.
These things are sacred.
Looking at that pot full of good soup,
I am thinking how in this simple manner,
The Great Spirit takes care of me.

This is a quiet and beautiful place: sounds of running water, canyon breezes, and the shrill cry of a hawk overhead. God's presence and goodness are close to me, there is no time, no further journey to make, only the enjoyment of this present moment.

My eyes gazed at the random pattern of shining obsidian chips in the sand at my feet. Then I saw the print. There it was front of me, on the game trail that the deer walk every morning and night. It was about three inches wide with a curved ridge between the four toes and the heel pad. There was no mistaking it: this was the print of a mountain lion. All around me were signs of deer, the lion's main source of protein. I imagined the lion slinking low through the brush nearby and then pouncing on the back of a deer, grasping the shoulder with its front claws, and biting the back of the neck to sever its spinal cord. (Cf. Rezendes, p.230)

I jumped off the rock and began to look around amidst the deer droppings. I found two mounds of large scat mixed with leaves –mountain lion scat. My observations suddenly became very personal. Across the ravine, thick with berry brambles, I thought I saw movement in the brush about fifty yards away. I thought I saw the golden yellow face of a large cat. A cold mantle of fear embraced me. My mouth became parched and I could hardly part my lips. What am I going to do?

It was time to go! I began walking slowly down the trail, then more rapidly. To my mind came the primeval injunction: *Don't feel fear! Animals sense when you are afraid.* I stopped and turned back towards the canyon. I tried to recall that pumped-up feeling before running out on the high school football field. I tried to think about John Wayne. But I felt shivers and my legs were shaking. I kept looking behind and around me. Now I need that gun!

Instinctively, I climbed out on one of the giant boulders. I stood up as high as I could and held my arms up in the air. I became as big as I could be and let out a loud roar with the full force of my lungs. The sound echoed up into the canyon. I continued to roar. I thought of Jan and Katie and Erik. I had to stay alive! Anger took me, and I yelled with all of my might and jumped up and down on the boulder.

Then, as suddenly as the fear had arisen, a strange calm came over me. Had I just blown off my terror? I looked around, threw a few rocks, and began walking down the trail back to the car, making lots of noise and looking behind me. Though no longer afraid, I *was* getting out of that place.

Living in Orange County, where the suburbs have been built all over pristine habitat, it is not unusual to hear of mountain lions and people coming in contact. Sacatar Canyon is mountain lion habitat too. This suggests that hiking here on your own has its risks. But is it any more dangerous than driving home on Highway 395, with those road demons from Mammoth breathing down my bumper?

Since 1986, there has been an increase in mountain lion attacks in this part of the world, with an average of one per year. The rate has increased since 1999. A support group for attack victims has been organized: California Lion Awareness (CLAW).

One writer shares:

So, we should be much more worried about meeting a car or the dogs we see every day rather than a mountain lion. Unfortunately, we aren't, because we are much more familiar with being in a car or being around a domestic dog than we are with being around an uncaged mountain lion. Rationally, if one avoids hiking because of fear of mountain lions, one should also avoid driving in a car, crossing a street as a pedestrian, or getting close to your own or someone else's dog... If you want to virtually eliminate any mountain lion danger to yourself, don't hike alone"

(Chester)

I asked a friend of mine, who hiked the Sierra Nevada and has a lot of wilderness experience, what he did to prevent encounters with bears and mountain lions. He told me that he ties a bell, the size of a quarter, on his backpack. This seems to let the creatures know that someone is coming. I went to the True Value Hardware Store in Lone Pine (they have everything) and bought the bell and tied it to my backpack. At least I feel better.

Mountain lions or not, as soon as I leave it, I long to return to Sacatur Canyon.

Listen to the air.
You can hear it, feel it,
Smell it, taste it.
Woniya wakan, the holy air,
Which renews all by its breath,
Woniya wakan, spirit, life, breath, renewal,
It means all that.
We sit together, don't touch,
But something is there,
We feel it between us,
As a presence.
A good way to start thinking about nature,
Talk about it.
Rather talk to it,
Talk to the rivers, to the lakes,
To the winds,
As to our relatives.

John Lame Deer (Steinmetz, p.38)

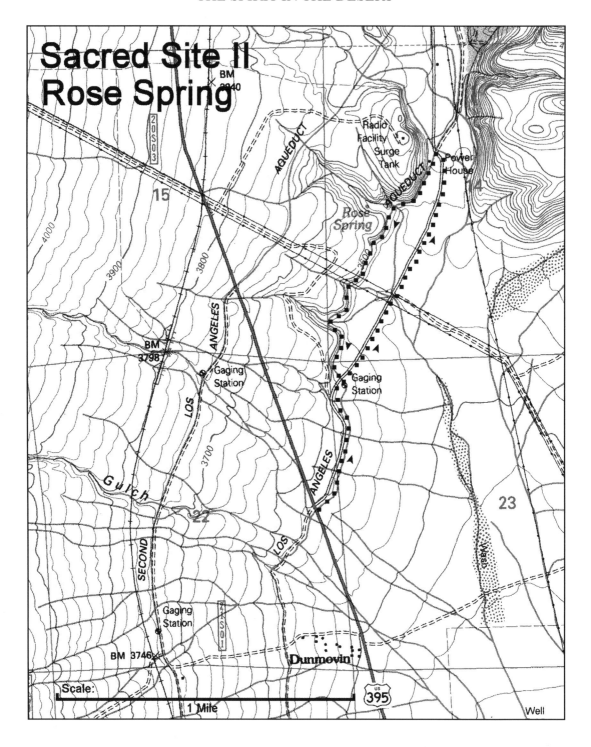

SACRED SITE II
ROSE SPRING:
GRAVES AND CAVES

The word 'pilgrimage' comes from the Latin pergrinus, which means 'stranger.' A pilgrim is someone who leaves the familiarity of home to become a stranger in a sacred place.

Mary Caswell

I searched through dozens of guidebooks, unable to find Rose Spring. But with the use of a topographic map and desert detective work, Rose Spring came into sight.

Traveling north on Highway 395, past Little Lake, Red Cinder Cone, and Coso Junction Rest Stop, the road will begin to gain elevation. Look for an abandoned settlement on the west side of the highway. This is, or was, Dunmovin.

Back in the early 1970's, the Reverend Canon Enrico Molnar, former Dean of Bloy House School of Theology, established a monastic community here. From the road you can see the individual cells or hermitages of his foundation. Canon Molnar was an extraordinary person; I remember that he spoke six languages, and took pains to know every saint's first, last and middle names and where he or she was born and conducted ministry. His illuminated manuscripts were so well executed that you would think they came straight out of a medieval monastery. He had been very active in diocesan programs until at one point in his life he began to experience visions of saints and of Jesus, which prompted him to leave institutional ministry and found a religious order. The community began here at Dunmovin and later moved to Chermainus, British Columbia.

Very quickly after Dunmovin, a sign indicates an intersection. Slow down. A sign for Haiwee Powerplant will appear, the road for which runs east. This exit comes quickly and is easy to miss. Take the exit and you will cross a cattle grate as you head east towards the trees and metal-roofed buildings. You will come to a locked gate with 'no trespassing' warning signs. The paved road ends here. This is the entry to one of the power plants and pump stations which direct water from the Haiwee Reservoir, just north of here, into the concrete-covered Second Los Angeles Aqueduct.

Continue to the left on a maintained dirt road. You will see the aqueduct running parallel to this road which will begin to curve back in the direction you came from. Look carefully to the north, or your right. Soon you will see a small canyon. A rocky cliff on the right will appear, with three distinct caves, easy to spot. When you see the caves, pull your car as far off the road to the right as you safely can, and park. You want to allow room for the Department of Water and Power maintenance trucks to get past you.

Leave your car and walk through the brush onto the covered aqueduct. Walk along it and note the little canyon. Do you see a rock cistern, surrounded by greenery, on the left side of the canyon wall? That is Rose Spring! Look carefully and you will see the stonework-reinforced dirt road going from left to right, on this side of the canyon. It slopes down directly to Rose Spring.

Rose Spring was a stage stop of the Mojave and Keeler Stage Line, between Little Lake Station and Olancha Station, on the way to the important silver mines of Cerro Gordo, whose riches built San Pedro Harbor and made Los Angeles into a city.

Walk the concrete aqueduct towards the stage road. You will see a pathway leading to the Spring. Before you walk down the path, get a feel for this space. Look north, up the little canyon. In the far distance you can make out the spillway of a dam which holds back the Haiwee Reservoir, the third collector of the waters of the Owens Valley. Nowadays the aqueduct leads the water to the thirsty homes of Los Angeles, but you can imagine the flow of an ancient river through this little canyon. The overflow from once deep Owens Lake passed through here, filling inland lakes many miles away, back into Death Valley. The best and safest times to visit here are late fall or early spring. In the spring abundant wildflowers grow in the sandy soil by the path.

Walk towards Rose Spring. You can see black, shiny chips of obsidian glittering on the ground. They tell you that you are hiking through what was once a Northern Paiute settlement, which reached its zenith of activity fifteen hundred years ago. As mentioned above, the significant local deposit of obsidian is found five miles east of Red Cinder Cone. There, Native Americans would cut large pieces of the mineral which they would carry to their camps. The pieces would be chipped into arrowheads, knives and scrapers, and also broken down into sizes easy to transport long distances. Anthropologists believe that this obsidian was a major trade resource. The trade routes went over the Sierra Nevada mountains, into the Central Valley, and as far as the seacoast. (Cf. Gilreath, 1997). Remember that artifacts are federally protected. If everyone took souvenirs, soon there would be nothing for others to appreciate. I like to inspect the edges of the obsidian chips to see if they have been flaked to create sharper edges. Imagine the centuries that have passed.

The vegetation becomes denser as you approach Rose Spring. The Rose Spring stage station was at the base of the Spring, the pile of large stones is what is left of the building. In 1868 the stationmaster's wife and son were killed here in an Indian raid and the station was burned. If you continue a little north, something else will appear out of the underbrush: the old concrete water troughs for the stage horses. Imagine the stagecoach arriving with silver- crazed miners in a big hurry, covered with dust, throats parched. Horses are watered and a fresh team is hooked up. Some passengers get out for a taste of the cold spring water.

Now look across the canyon to the face of the rocky cliff. You saw the caves when you left your car. Walk toward the cliff face. This was the site of several archeological excavations by the University of California at Berkeley, beginning in 1957.

The Native Americans who lived in this little canyon were a band of the Coso branch of Northern Paiutes. As you look south toward Little Lake you see Rose Valley. To the right, up against the Sierra, is a ledge formation called Portuguese Bench. Little Lake, Portuguese Bench and Rose Spring are ancient Native American sites dating back several thousand years.

Michael Delacourt, of Caltrans., CSU Sacramento, reports that the Native Americans of Rose Spring belong to the Haiwee Period:

41

The onset of the Haiwee Period (AD 650-1350) seems to mark the beginnings of a set of dramatic changes that were to take place in Owens Valley. Projectile point shapes include smaller Eastgate and Rose Springs forms. On account of their smaller size, these forms have generally been taken as markers of the introduction of bow-and-arrow technology. Lith assemblages from Haiwee sites are characterized by high proportions of expedient and casual flake stone tools, which seem to have replaced bifaces as the primary cutting and scraping tools. The use of extra-local obsidian sources almost disappears from the record, with local sources dominating both formal tools and debitage profiles, suggesting a highly restricted and centralized mobility pattern. Faunal remains, especially at residential sites (e.g. Rose Springs), are typically more diverse and are dominated by small to medium sized mammals and birds, and occasionally freshwater shellfish. These species, which can be procured in large quantities, hint at an intensification on certain key food resources during Haiwee times, especially low-ranked items. There is further evidence that Haiwee settlement patterns were modified in order to take advantage of these resources, as settlements were located next to or right on procurement spots.

When the Berkeley archeologists dug below three feet, they began to find plenty of evidence that Rose Spring had been a Northern Paiute home for a long time. The students and professors had to carefully screen great quantities of material, thus large piles of screened sand accumulated, which accounts for the mounds at the base of the cliff. Among the items found were lots of arrowheads, knives and scrapers, and some pottery–which may have come through trade with the Anazasis of Arizona. The most important find was located below several of the piles of rocks that you will see in the excavation area: about seven feet down, three distinct graves were uncovered. One of these was of a fourteen year-old boy who had been buried in a deerskin shirt, sewn with small seashells which had been brought hundreds of miles across the mountains from what is now the coastal city of Santa Barbara.

Other famous archeological sites in this area include Little Lake (paleo-Indian period) and Cottonwood (AD 1350–1850).

Continue walking along the cliff, back in the direction of the road. You are now walking toward the three caves. Two of the caves will be easier to spot. With caution, you can climb up to them through the rocks. They are not very deep, but you can see that they would have provided some shelter. The third cave is larger and is reached by climbing up about twenty feet of rock debris to the left of the two shallower caves.

I first entered this cave during the time of another health crisis for our then fourteen year-old son, Erik. As I climbed the rocky shelf towards the entrance, a large white Great Horned Owl flew out. The surprise almost caused me to fall. Immediately I remembered that for some Native Americans the owl is a sign of imminent death. I thought again about the grave of the fourteen year-old Paiute boy. Inside the cave, I could see the owl's nest high up in the roof. I turned and looked out over the canyon. I could see for miles toward the south, to Little Lake and the entrance to Owens Valley. This would have been a superb lookout for the Paiute.

I sat on a rock within the cave and the spiritual numbness I had been feeling all these months with Erik's sickness welled up in me. At times like this I find a spiritual anchor in reading scripture aloud. The words seem more alive and personal that way. I stood again at the mouth of the cave and opened the Bible to this passage in which the prophet Elijah Meets God at Horeb:

> He said, 'Go out and stand on the mountain before the Lord, for the Lord is about to pass by.' Now there was a great wind, so strong that it was splitting mountains and breaking rocks in pieces before the Lord, but the Lord was not in the wind; and after the wind an earthquake, but the Lord was not in the earthquake; and after the earthquake a fire, but the Lord was not in the fire; and after the fire a sound of sheer silence. When Elijah heard it, he wrapped his face in his mantle and went out and stood at the entrance of the cave. Then there came a voice to him that said, 'What are you doing here, Elijah?'

> I Kings 19:11-13

Harvard Chaplain Peter Gomes preached a sermon on this text: *The Question at the Mouth of the Cave.*

> Elijah comes to the cave at a terrible low point of inward fear and doubt. His career as a prophet of God has been very successful, but Elijah is alone, defeated, fearful and faithless.

> Elijah has fled to this cave out of fear for Jezebel's threats to have him killed. The cave to which he fled expressed where Elijah was in his life at that point. A cave is 'a depression in unyielding rock that gives for a while apparent security and protection.'

The popular prophet Elijah holds up in a cave in his depression and panic.

As we read the story, the Lord asks Elijah, "What are you doing here, Elijah?" "Nothing at all," is the reply.

Here the prophet of Israel learns his second lesson, for if the first lesson is that failure is often the price of success, the second is that 'being in God' rather than 'doing for God' is the ultimate sign of faithfulness.

Here again is the spiritual challenge for men. We see even the call to spiritual life with God as a work project and task. We can become self-critical about 'praying right' and lists of spiritual disciplines. We read books about spirituality (or we write them!) When we are tired, sufficiently exhausted, emotionally numb, or at the end of our rope, we stop doing and we can 'be', we can rest in the Lord."

(Gomes, 1998)

We may seek God in the flash of notable events, sparkling and insightful wisdom, peak experiences, but Elijah's witness in the cave is for us. It is in the heart, in the stillness, silence and solitude that we hear the soft voice of God. This is the presence of Abba Father that Jesus himself met in the desert. And Jesus wants us to know this Presence to be closer than our own breathing.

I stand at the mouth of the cave, astonished at the vista before me, feeling a numb emptiness in the pit of my stomach, and wondering why I have to drive this far into the wilderness in order to quiet the priest's mental jungle of projects and 'to do lists' for God. I am grateful that God's voice invites me to listen to the loving sounds of sweetness. Indeed, in this cave, I can rest in the Lord.

After you have visited the caves, walk through the sandy brush as best you can to the foot of the stage road. Walk up the incline of the stage road and notice as you walk higher the natural flow of the watercourse before there was a road and aqueduct. The stage road will continue around a bend and head toward the Sierra Nevada mountains. Within 100 yards, the ground will level out a little. Look to your right for low-lying rocks. You will find a well-preserved Indian grinding stone with several well-worn mortars. These impressions were created after many years of grinding seeds such as the pinyon pine nut, which were a protein staple. I found a more substantial set of nine grinding holes in a rock about 100 yards northwest toward the hill. Each hole was 'owned' by a woman in the tribe, who also passed it on to her daughter.

As you walk further to your right, away from the stage road, you will see a vast open area on the top of the Rose Spring bluff. Scattered over several acres are thousands of obsidian chips. Fifteen hundred years ago this was a busy factory for cutting large blocks of obsidian from the Coso deposit into smaller sections that could be carried south, north and west for trade with other tribes. Can you imagine the village: the cone-shaped reed huts, the women talking and grinding at the rock, the children laughing and playing, and the sound of the men chipping the stones?

You can return to your car via the stage road. Continue on the dirt road as it circles back to the paved road. Watch carefully for the paved road, turn right and you will come back to 395. Enter the highway very carefully, as it is a divided highway at this point. Turn right and you will be heading north to Lone Pine.

Author and Paiute grinding stone with nine grinding holes. 2006. Photograph: Janice Karelius.

Paiute dwelling, Owens Valley, c.1890. Photograph: Eastern California Museum.

Rose Springs, excavation of Paiute graves by the University of California at Berkeley, 1957. Photograph: Bancroft Library.

AN ADVENT CONVERSATION WITH GOD

Holy God,
You are never far
from those who seek you.
Be our companion on our
Lenten journey.
Guide us out of our slavery,
our addictions,
our less-than-ultimate concerns.
Lead us to sacred places
and holy people.
Be our strength.
Revive the weary,
protect our young,
shelter the homeless,
re-orient the lost.
Divine origin, be our destination.
We ask this through Christ our Lord.
Amen.

A Blessing For Pilgrims

I wrote what follows in this chapter after the first visit to Rose Spring and during another health crisis with Erik. I thought I would include it here because it gives some idea of what fostered in me the great and continuing need to become a desert pilgrim. Whether we admit it or not, no-one is immune from the feeling that at some point God's grace is distant or withheld. It certainly appeared that way to me: there was anguish about a loved one, a feeling of isolation from friends and family, a collapse of my ambitions. In the Christian calendar, Advent is the period of four weeks before Christmas; a time of preparation, penance, and reflection. And a time to get personal with God.

The southern California heat is diminishing. Finally, autumn days have come with a cool wind and a gentle, moist and foggy cast to the mornings. And the darkness is coming.

Come, Lord Jesus.

As I come to darkening Advent days, O Lord, I come into your presence with persistent apprehension. Our dear Erik is thin and diminished himself. I am afraid he will not live until Christmas.

On a Wednesday in early October, I drive south on Interstate 5, from my parish in Santa Ana to Mission Hospital in Mission Viejo. I am pushing 80 mph and there are no flashing red lights behind me. My mind moves between panic and hope. Our fourteen year-old Erik has finally been admitted to Pediatric ICU. My wife Jan is with him now. I must get there. What will I see?

We have lived with a series of crises for Erik over the last ten years, since his healthy life was forever changed by encephalitis. During the last three months, Erik has been severely anorexic. The new anti-seizure drug, Topomax, among the handful of drugs he takes three times a day, has caused him neither to want to drink nor eat. We hoped the drug would help his daily seizures and the neurologist held-off cutting the drug. But Erik at five-feet-ten has dropped from 138 pounds to 112. He has not eaten anything for eight days and retains minimal fluid.

I arrive at Erik's bed to see the nurse and Jan beside him. IV fluids drip at rapid pace. He has a glassy, unfocused gaze. He does not speak or recognize me. The breathing monitor alarm sounds every few minutes. Erik's respiration is between nine and eleven per minute, and dropping. He stops breathing. The alarm sounds again. Jan tells him to breathe. He is so exhausted from the long bouts of retching and vomiting that breathing is very difficult.

Your grace is with me, O Lord. I am present to this.

The last thing Jan needs is my anxiety and questions. Jan and I and the nurse talk softly, though we are ever-vigilant about Erik's breathing.

Lord, are you wrestling with the Angel of Death for us?

One minute, I want Erik's suffering over, even if it means his death–and I feel very guilty about having this idea–the next minute, the smallest improvement is magnified into hope. What is real is only this present moment. Erik's breath. In and out. Very slow. Laboring. Not the breath before, not the next breath. Only this present breath. You are here, Jesus. You hold Jan and me and Erik in your loving embrace. If Erik stops breathing or breaths once again, you are here.

> Since, therefore the children share flesh and blood, he himself likewise shared the same things, so that through death he might destroy the one who has the power of death, that is, the devil, and free those who all their lives were held in slavery by the fear of death. Because he himself was tested by what he suffered, he is able to help those who are being tested.

> Hebrews 2:9-18

I see, O Lord, your suffering on the cross. You are here. You know his laboring for breath and his suffering. I am helpless. My mind struggles for control, imagining scenarios of possible outcomes for Erik and matching my emotions to the scenarios. More attempts at control. I will go through this until my mind stops, and again I must surrender to you, here and now in Erik's breathing.

The IV drips. Urine passes. After three hours the breathing improves and there are no monitor alarms. There is no time or agenda for the future, only the present, with Jan and I and Erik, and now our twenty-one year-old daughter, Katie, who has joined us.

Jan and I have tried to create a plan for each day of crisis leading up to now. But every day there are new symptoms, and Erik has been declining. Every day the plan changes. Now we live one day at a time. My overscheduled calendar of 'important things' is suddenly triaged, and from somewhere a helpful voice inquires: *do you really have to be doing this right now?* I refocus on where I need to be, with Erik and the family.

Two weeks ago, Erik's difficulty in holding food and fluids began to grow worse. I had been on the edge of tears. Waves of sadness crashed over me as I tried to present a calm, strong presence for the family. Then I visited a parishioner with multiple sclerosis, and my feelings started to leak out. That same evening, at prayers with the Vestry before our meeting, I asked for healing for Erik, and my emotions bubbled over and I fell apart. "I feel so helpless," I cried out. I don't think anyone in the parish had ever heard me say that before. The Vestry appeared around me, surrounding me in a holy huddle of prayer and laying on of hands. The fear and anxiety left me quickly.

And now, ten years later, it is hard for me to talk with parishioners about all those devastating events and my emotional response. I don't want to talk about Erik's health any more because people will think I am using it as a excuse for not doing my job. The people of Messiah Parish must be really tired of my roller-coaster family life–the phrase, 'compassion fatigue' springs to mind. Sensing disinterest, I keep my troubles from them. We have our family therapist and I have a spiritual director, and Jan and I have a few close friends with whom to share the burden. (She is much more open about her feelings). It is understandable that people get tired of the years of crisis.

Then there is the problem with the communication chain in the parish. Information about one crisis with Erik will slowly unfold and disseminate. People with old information will ask about a past crisis, and, as soon as I say that everything is better, we are dealing with another, which I don't want to talk about because people are still processing the old one.

On the Sunday before Erik went into ICU in Mission Viejo, Messiah Parish hosted a Mass of healing and remembrance for people affected by auto-immune deficiency syndrome (AIDS), the sufferers and family and friends. My mind was not working as I tried to prepare a meaningful liturgy in my role as Dean of the central Orange County congregations. My thoughts were entirely on Erik. I could not find anyone else to preach. It had to be me, but I did not want the focus on myself. I prayed: *God, how will you use me in this worship and also heal Erik and our family?*

The liturgy was set within a Requiem Eucharist: there were some hymns and prayers from the burial service, but the dominant theme was Easter and power of the Resurrection of Jesus. The small congregation consisted of persons I knew who had lost loved ones to AIDS and a few persons with AIDS.

The time came for the sermon. I had a few words of outline, but had no real idea what I would say. I took the crucifix from my office wall and held onto it as I began the sermon. I described an experience of the cross during the Good Friday Liturgy of the previous year. For twenty-five years of priesthood, I had preached about the cross. That Holy Week, leading up to Good Friday, I had prayed for the grace to know the suffering of Jesus. I shared in the sermon what God revealed to me. I saw Jesus on the cross in the church, and I focused on his heart. And I brought forth all of my worst fears about Erik: suffering in a lingering illness that would waste his body, or life as an adult in a group home, where, neglected, he withdraws into a slow decline. I saw Jesus enfolding Erik with his strong, pierced arms. All of my inexpressible visions of powerlessness in helping Erik were projected onto the sacred heart of Jesus on the cross.

Most of the congregation came forward for the anointing of the sick and laying on of hands. There was a powerful sense of the presence of the Holy Spirit and the power of the Resurrection. And I came forth to another holy huddle of prayer and anointing.

That first day in Pediatric ICU had been touch and go, but by evening Erik began to wake up. The hydration was improving and the eternal nausea subsided as the toxic drug worked its way out of his body. The next day, Jan walked into the room with a Del Taco soft drink cup. Erik grabbed it out of her hand and began to drink. This was the first time in three months that Erik had taken a drink of his own volition.

We took Erik home. I was worried that we were rushing his discharge, but Jan was determined to do the nursing at home. Two days later, he began to vomit again and it was back to the emergency room for more testing of the seizure medication levels. There were more phone calls to the pediatrician and the neurologists. And there was a growing awareness that the professionals did not know what was going on.

Erik is better. He is worse. He is better. He is sick again. People ask how he is. Old news cycles with the most recent. It is all a blur and I am tired of giving updates.

Where are you God? Are you listening to our cries, as Erik suffers? He does not cry. He expresses no fears or anxiety. Only the discomfort and pain of this present moment.

Then God answers my prayer again.

My friend, Tonnie Katz, is editor of the newspaper, The Orange County Register. Without my knowing it, she arranged a meeting between me and her friend, Rabbi Harold Kushner, who wrote the famous book, *Why Bad Things Happen to Good People.* The opportunity arose because he would be in San Diego to promote another book, *How Good Do You Have to Be?*

Dr. Kushner and I began to talk, and quickly I sensed we were on common ground. What a difference it makes to talk with someone who knows! Kushner's own son had died twenty years before, at the age of fourteen. It was clear that the wisdom he shared came not from his head, but from a heart that had known suffering. His wisdom was centered in faith in a loving God and the movement of God's amazing grace.

"I have a hard time sharing my feelings," I said. "When I try to share with people in the church, it usually seems as though the person doesn't want to hear what I am saying."

"Our situation is harder for some congregants to handle than for others," said Rabbi Kushner. "Draw nearer to those who do seem to care and are responsive to you. These are the people to spend time with."

Then I said, "When we are within another health crisis, and death is possible for Erik, I feel guilty about considering his death as a release. It seems that I want him to die for *me* to be released. What a terrible thought to have!"

"Cherish the times you have. Each one of them. Be present with him when you are there," said Rabbi Kushner. I recalled sitting on Erik's bed, rubbing his feet, and him saying, "I like it!" I recalled telling Erik a story in which he is the active character. ('This is communion,' wrote Jean Vanier).

Then I said to Dr. Kushner, "I wonder how it will be when he dies. As I go through this time with Jan and Katie, I feel like I am under inspection, as if there are some standards of appropriate behavior that I especially am supposed to hold, and something in me wants to react angrily, 'inappropriately' to this perception."

"No one can predict how they will feel, when we face death", Kushner advised. "But the support will be there for us, if we will look for it."

I consider the times when God's grace has seen me through a previous crisis in my life, in my marriage, or with Erik. I act as though I expect to have saved up enough grace to get me through the next event. But I cannot save up grace. If I could save up enough grace to meet the next unknown, then I do not need God. I am never far from my need for God. Remember the phrase, 'Sufficient is the grace for the moment?' I pray for the grace to again trust God's goodness: that God will be there as always before.

During our conversation, Kushner said something that has stayed with me and is seen throughout his writings: "We ask: 'God, where are you in this suffering? Speak to me!' Martin Buber said: 'Humans are God's language.' Look for the surprising, miraculous movements of God's grace with the people who are with you in this time."

Lord, this is true. You have sent to us a caring and skilled neurologist and a pediatrician and family therapist. You have planted me among a supportive congregation.

This Advent, as we move into days that darken early, looking for the grace and miracle of God's hand in the world, I pray for the grace to get away from narcissistic feelings and experiences and to be drawn more to Christ, to embrace his cross as the way that leads to full life with God and to place on that cross my worst fears –which I cannot even describe in words.

I want to place that fear-filled darkness on the hard wood of Jesus' cross and I want to ask Jesus to guide me to those people who will walk the way of the cross with me: Jan, Katie and Erik.

I look back on these ten years of unbelievable change for our family. Erik would have started high school last month, had he been a 'normal' child. I look back on six years of intensive, compulsive, ambition-driven interviewing for a new parish or diocesan position, building on what I had the chutzpah to call 'my success' as an inner city rector. Now I can see God's hand, God's movement more clearly through those six years of excruciating and sometimes abusive interviews. God's dream was that as we walk the way of the cross, our family would be anchored in a congregation that does care about us and wants the very best for us. I find now that I am working in a congregation that has become my ideal. If I had taken up a new position, I would doubtless be intensely busy with new projects, and allowing Jan to bear the brunt of this current crisis with Erik.

I am rooted in this place, this home, this congregation, this community, and this family. And with my quaking, shaking feet standing on faith, I look for the movement of God's amazing grace.

Author with son, Erik. Picnic at Briar Creek, south of Manzanar, 1997. Janice Karelius.

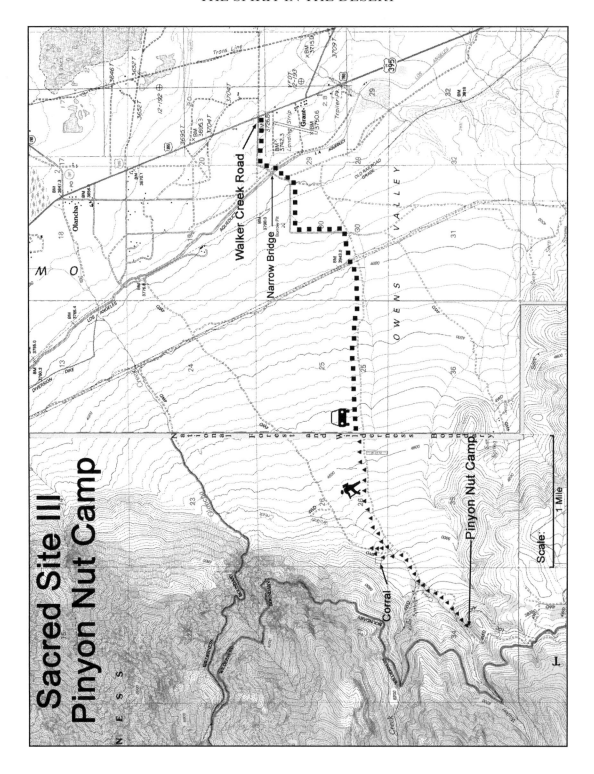

SACRED SITE III
PINYON NUT CAMP

But a tree is what you make of it, and once, much was made of the pinyon.

Ronald Lanner

I have leaned heavily on the research of other people in writing this chapter. The scene is beautifully set for my Advent 2002 pilgrimage by Michael Delacourt of California State University at Sacramento. This is his description of the Seasonal Cycle of the Owens Valley Paiute:

Winter
Like most people who live close to the land, the Owens Valley Paiute structured their lives around the wild plants and animals they used as food. These were found in different places throughout the year, taking the people from the banks of the Owens River to the wind-swept mountains as seasons changed. Winters were usually spent in villages on the valley floor, where people lived in pole and brush winter houses. Food came from stored seeds and nuts collected in the summer and fall. Ducks, rabbits, and other animals were hunted and time was spent visiting friends, telling stories and making baskets and other equipment and tools.

Spring

Early spring was often a hard time. Stored food was running low and the first of the new crops had yet to sprout. Some of the first edible plants were the tender shoots of wild onion, watercress, and cat-tail. These were collected near winter villages until other food was available.

As melting snow filled the Owens River, fish and freshwater mussels were caught and eaten, and the seeds of many plants were gathered and stored. Some of these food remains are preserved in archaeological sites and tell us what the people ate.

Artifacts such as grinding stones and arrowheads tell us where and how prehistoric people lived in the valley. The information these artifacts contain is priceless and that is why they are protected by State and Federal law.

Summer

When the grass began to dry, families often traveled by themselves to collect seeds. Others went high into the mountains to gather roots and to hunt mountain sheep, marmots, and rabbits.

Life in the mountains was difficult. The rugged high country was cold and had little firewood. Houses had to be warm. Their sturdy rock foundations can still be seen today.

Fall

As the days grew shorter and the rose-hips turned red, people knew that the pinyon pine nuts were ripe. These were an important food, and families from all over the valley went to the mountains to gather nuts for the winter. Everyone helped. Children climbed into the trees to shake the loose nuts free, while their parents and grandparents picked the sticky green cones from high branches with long hooked poles.

If only a few weeks were spent in the mountains, people lived in simple brush shelters. If families decided to stay longer, they would build a sturdy house of logs.

Most families returned to the valley after the pinyon harvest. This was a happy time. The days were still warm, there was plenty to eat, and many friends to visit after the long summer. A festival was usually organized at Bishop, Big Pine, or another village. There were games, dances, news to share, and communal rabbit or antelope hunts. When the festival was over, people went home to their villages to prepare for winter, starting the cycle again.

Pine Nut gathering, Owens Valley c. 1930. Author's collection.

We had to take Erik to the emergency room again because he has been vomiting non-stop. We think it is a high Felbatol level (one of his seizure medications), but it is a guessing game –the blood test results take several days. We make a decision to lower the dose and I have to detach from my deep desire to make the retreat to the Pinyon Nut Camp. After an anxious day, Erik stabilizes and I decide to make the journey after all.

It is a beautiful bright Monday in November. Snow has fallen over the Sierra. The weather is supposed to be mild but windy. I decide to explore what for me is a new way into the Walker Creek-Olancha Creek area. Driving south on 395, past the Ranch House Restaurant in Olancha, I look for Walker Creek Road. There is a very small street sign on the right indicating a well-traveled dirt road, which I take, (it appears to be leading to a desert burro protection reserve). I come to a very narrow bridge over the aqueduct, but my 2000 Oldsmobile Bravada has enough room to cross. I set my sights on the grove of pinyon pines in the distant canyon, on Walker Creek. The road has some rough spots, but a mid-size passenger car would not have too much difficulty here.

I decide to park at the large cluster of boulders on the right, just before the boundary sign announcing that I have entered a National Forest. That is a good idea, because the road becomes rough after that point –probably Level III for four-wheel drive.

Walking on the road, I take a fork to the right, which passes through the rushing waters of Walker Creek. On the other side there is a corral that was once used for pack horses and mules. Littered about the ground are the remains of old beehives.

Returning to the original dirt road, I head toward the pinyon pine grove. What a day! Golden, shimmering leaves, mild temperature, bright sun, rushing water, and I am totally alone.

When I arrive at the pinyon pine grove I break out lunch and find a good flat rock upon which to rest. As I look around, I remember that the Owens Valley Paiute visited the pinyon forests at about this time for the annual harvest. The yield of the harvest directly affected the health of the tribe, as pinyon nuts were a principle source of protein which could be stored in basket caches for many months. This lowly, dwarf, scrub conifer was a tree of great importance to the people of the Great Basin. Ronald Lanner writes in his wonderful book, *The Piñon Pine:*

This little tree produced the fuel, building materials, food, and medicines that enabled prehistoric Indians to establish their cultures on the Colorado Plateau—and to survive into the present as Hopi, Zuni, Pueblo and Navajo. It was the piñon that made the Great Basin the coarse-grained Eden of the pine-nut eaters who picked their winter sustenance from the treetops.

As I walk about these acres, I can see areas where brush has been cleared for sleeping space. Over there is the remains of a large, hooked pole which was used for pulling down the cones.

The gathering process involved the whole Paiute community. Cones were harvested when they were still green (before animals would get at them). They were heated and gathered in blankets. The heat would open the cones and the blankets would catch the seeds. It was a messy business with lots of sticky pitch. The precious pine nuts were eventually roasted and parceled out to families, as they prepared for the harsh, cold winter. Just as the buffalo sustained the Plains Indians, the pinyon pinenut was God's gift to the Paiutes. It is a wonderfood, containing all twenty amino-acids. The Paiutes could harvest up to two hundred and fifty pounds of nuts from an acre of forest. The sacred pinenut is a storehouse of concentrated nutrition with a high protein content, making the pinyon a substantial contributor to Paiute nutrition and survival.

Sitting here in this place of beauty, I imagine the Paiute families gathering in the fall. The long summer of little water and sparse food is over. The air is cooling and they come to this place anticipating an end to their chronic hunger. The children run about shrieking and laughing as the men reach up high to the pinecone-laden boughs. They beat the branches with long poles and the cones fall among circles of playing children. They praise the Great Spirit for sustaining them through another year.

In these clan gatherings, families catch up with the news from other clans up and down the valley. There will be dancing, gambling, and romance will flower. There is much joy as they tell about babies born, and there will be a Cry Dance for those who have died. Because of the large number of people who come together in the pinyon gathering, there will be a communal rabbit hunt. Rabbitskin blankets provide warmth in the coming winter.

A Pinenut Chief chooses the place for the festivities. Each year the harvest varies: the big harvests may be every third year or every seventh. The Pinenut Chief has to be someone with a lot of wisdom about the harvesting process. He needs to know how to read the signs. Pinyon pinecones take three years to mature. The clans will have noticed the budding growth at the end of the first summer. In the spring, tiny cones could be seen. After fertilization and by August of the second year, these new cones would be six-inches long and bright purple. If there are a lot of purple cones, that will be the location selected by the Pinenut Chief for the following year.

By the third summer, sticky black pitch drips from the shiny green knobs of the ripe cones and soon the cones dry and turn brown. Then the scales of the cones begin to open like flowers, two pine nuts in each scale. But the nuts do not fall out by themselves. By October, before the squirrels and bluejays find the ripe nuts, the people will have gathered for the harvest. For three nights there will be dances. One of the songs sung to the beating of drums celebrates the sustaining, holy land:

How beautiful is our land
How beautiful is our land
Forever, beside the water, the water
How beautiful is our land
How beautiful is our land
How beautiful is our land
Earth with flowers on it, next to the water
How beautiful is our land.

While the families awaken to the morning of the fourth day, breakfast fires already smoking, the Pine Nut Chief offers a prayer to the Great Spirit that the harvest will be a good one. The people wash themselves before they begin, for this is holy work. The cones are harvested in the cool morning before the day's heat causes the pinyon sap to drip.

Men form hooks out of small branches which they attach to long willow poles. Working in twos and threes, the men guide each other in knocking down the cones from the laden boughs. Twigs and cones and pitch all fall to the ground. The children, scurrying to collect the sticky cones, become covered in the dark pitch; in the evening they will have to roll in the dust before going to sleep under their rabbitskin blankets. Women pile the cones into willow baskets which they carry on their backs with deerskin cords across their foreheads. It is hard work for everyone.

Then the ripe pinecones are dumped into rock-lined pits. They are covered with dirt and a fire is kindled above. In the evening, as the older women prepare a meal, the cooking pits are opened. The heat from the fire has burst open the cones and cooked the pinenuts. The pinenuts are collected and some are stored in deerskin bags for use later in the year. Split willow winnowing baskets, shaped like giant spoons, are filled with the remaining cooked pinenuts. The piles of nuts are flipped into the air and the wind takes up the refuse of broken shells.

Now the pinenuts are ready to be placed on flat stones and the women use grinding stones with light pressure to break open the hard, cooked shells, being careful not to crush the pinenuts. These grinding stones will stay here in the camp, stowed away under brush or between rocks to be used when the harvest comes to this area again.

The pinenuts can be eaten right away but the common practice is to grind them up into a fine grey powder. The women make thick pinenut gravy which tastes of pinesap and wood smoke. The Paiutes eat this as a soup with berries or use it as gravy over meat. On cold winter days, mothers freeze leftover pinenut gravy and the children eat it like ice cream. And, if this is a year of abundant harvest, the clans will spend the winter in the pinyon grove, whole, well-fed and satisfied. (Cf. 'Pinenut,' Great Basin College).

In this place of holy abundance where I imagine echoes of drums and dancing songs, I remember the voices of the Jewish people in the Psalm:

> The eyes of all wait on thee: and thou givest them their meat in due season.
> Thou openest thine hand and satisfiest the desire of every living thing.

Psalm 145:15-16

I come away to this desert land and sit on a granite rock in the shade of the pinyon grove. The only sound is the wind blowing through the thick pine boughs. A fat, dark pinecone falls at my feet.

Afterwards, I drive back to Lone Pine, go into Joseph's Market and walk to the produce section in the back where I find a large bag of pine nuts. As I hold this precious bag in my hand and wait in line at the checkout counter, the sounds of drumming and singing echo in my ears.

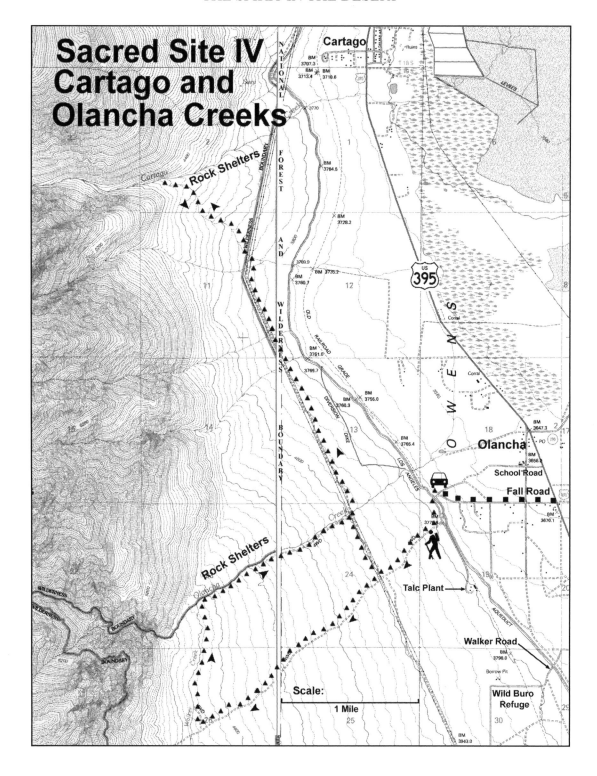

SACRED SITE IV
CARTAGO, OLANCHA AND
WALKER CREEKS

All things are taken up and become whole in contemplation. One does not have to waste time sorting them, grading them, evaluating them. They are there as reality and that is that.

Thomas Merton, *New Seeds of Contemplation*

This journey to a source of abundant life in the desert and some ancient Native American rock shelters is another that took place around the time of Advent. I concentrated my meditation hikes to the east of the little town of Olancha which lies between Highway 395 and the Sierra Nevada. For thousands of years this area was sacred to the Owens Valley Paiute.

Olancha is a verdant oasis on Highway 395, near the southwestern edge of Owens Lake. Anglos first settled here in the 1860's when the little town became the Wells Fargo stage stop after Rose Spring. A few years later, Olancha became an important beef raising center and a supply point for the big silver mines of Cerro Gordo. Driving to Olancha in the summer, with temperatures over 100°F, you look on the huge old cottonwoods that line the road as heavenly green umbrellas—they are sweet protection from the penetrating sun. In the winter, the trees are stark and barren, in the autumn, their leaves are shimmering gold.

My favorite stop for rest and refreshment is in Olancha, on the west side of the road, at the Ranch House Cafe. It is imbued with cowboy culture and ranch life. When I had lunch here last year, a group of cowboys entered, spurs jingling loudly, taking a break from weaning calves from their mothers. More often than not you will hear conversations in French and German as Europeans love this place. The owners of this restaurant, Herman and Claudine Meylemans, are Belgian, and Herman is a *cordon bleu* chef. My favorite lunch at their establishment is ranch beans, cornbread and hot coffee, and my customary table is on the north side of the building where I can gaze out the window at grazing cattle.

Look to the Sierra Nevada, rising in the west. You can see the canyons below which have been carved by creeks fed with snowmelt. At the mouth of every one of these canyons a Northern Paiute village once flourished, each organized under its own chief or headman. In the foothill area beginning at Olancha and northward to Cottonwood, was one of the largest contiguous populations of Paiutes.

The foothills beckon, and despite the allure of the Ranch House, I know I must be on my way.

As you continue north on 395, leaving Olancha, you will pass some modern blue buildings. There are windows facing the highway where you can stop and see what is going on inside. This is the bottling plant for the famous Crystal Geyser waters that you and I drink, the water sources being Cartago Creek and Olancha Creek. But just before the bottling plant there is an entrance to a ranch on the east side of the highway. Park your vehicle opposite, on the west side of the highway. Of the several ways to get to Cartago Creek, this is going to be a challenging hike, one of the most difficult that I will describe.

There are several trails heading west. I look for the railroad tracks of the abandoned Southern Pacific 'Jawbone' Line, which originate in Mojave. I find an underpass where I can walk under the track. On the other side flows the aqueduct which, being uncovered at this point, is protected by a long fence. A dirt maintenance road runs along the eastern bank of the waterway. The challenge is to get across the water to continue the hike to Cartago Creek. But this is a 'no trespassing' area and I decide to search elsewhere for my route.

For easier and safer access to this area, drive south on Highway 395 through Olancha. Look for Fall Road, it comes just after School Road. Turn right on the paved road and drive west toward the Sierra. You will come to the old right-of-way of the Southern Pacific Railroad line to Lone Pine. The road bears left toward a talc plant. Turn your vehicle around and park outside the fence, near the residential area. As you walk back through the fence, over the old railroad bed and the bridge over the aqueduct, look for the dirt road heading for the Sierra. You can walk this road all the way to Walker Creek, which is an interesting and beautiful detour that will climb about one thousand feet.

I had searched for this creek on three previous hikes, but kept missing it. Now I have another map, and am reoriented, and hope that I am on the right path. The elevation increases rapidly. I come upon the very dry bed of Walker Creek. I continue climbing toward a healthy grove of green pinyon pines whose forbears sustained the people who once made their lives here. I think I hear something. I keep walking and then I stop and listen some more. It isn't the wind. What is it? I walk over to the creek—and there is abundant rushing water.

After another hour of uphill hiking, I reach the pinyon pine grove which, up close, is more a forest. Walker Creek is still on my right. I stop for lunch and a long rest, sitting on a large flat boulder. My heartbeat and labored breath slow down and I am able to take in the expansive space. Next to me Walker Creek splashes over a waterfall. Golden cottonwood and aspen trees crowd the banks of the creek and their luminescent leaves shimmer in the slight breeze. Have you ever seen a view so beautiful that it hurts? My mind is empty of thoughts and agenda and worries. I feel totally in the present moment, rejoicing in this beauty and filled with wonder and gratitude to the One who made all of this. In silence and solitude, God's loving, caring presence envelops me.

This desert wilderness, which can seduce us with its beauty and majesty, has many faces. The desert is a place of wonder and exploration, a place of rest and renewal. That is, until you get lost in it. Then the desert can be a place of dread and terror, where you need survival skills or you can die: good maps, plenty of water, pace yourself. And you need God.

And there, on my beautiful boulder, heartbeat slowing, I think of what it means to survive in the rest of my life: I think about driving the freeway every morning and plunging into routine with endless tasks and the needs of other people. I think: *It's a desert out there.* Those with survival skills will make it.

It is clear that the survival skills I need are not so much to do with self-reliance, as with regular, daily communion with Jesus and the Word of God. I remember the want of survival skills of the Jewish people in the Exodus: there was nothing they could do on their own to find food and water. Casting themselves on God's grace, they were led from water hole to water hole, and were fed with manna.

There is a voice calling to me, the voice of One who knew me before I was born and who calls me by name. I walk through the deserts of my life. Though I look for a bridge over this chasm and a safe path through that quicksand, I know I cannot trust my own senses or rely on directions that are not God's. My false self is always deceptive, leading me down barren paths to addiction and self-destruction.

I want to trust the voice of God that I hear in this desert—my directional signals. *Go forward, take a risk. Stop and take a rest and think about what is going on here. Turn around and come back to the right road.*

Speaking about the right road, it is quite possible to get to Olancha Creek without all this climbing. You take a right-hand path after the bridge over the aqueduct and head towards the tree-lined area in the distance. I remember stunning days in the fall, walking Olancha Creek, aspen and cottonwood shimmering yellow and gold and the water rushing in a vast arid landscape.

The area of the three creeks is strewn with huge boulders. Most of them are situated on the sides of Cartago Creek. As they bunch together, and you walk among them, you will notice obsidian chips and other signs of settlement: small, ancient rock walls. You will be able to identify old rock shelters of the Paiutes, who lived along this creek for many centuries. I have seen stone scrapers, knives and other artifacts within the crevices of these ancient rock shelters. If you see them, leave them for the next person to appreciate. Imagine the lives of the extended families who lived here in a Stone Age culture, before the invasion of the Anglo-Europeans in the 1860's.

This whole area between Walker Creek, Olancha Creek and Cartago Creek is where the Paiutes gathered for major religious ceremonies. It is sacred space. As I move through this vast expanse in walking mediation, I lose track of time. (When eventually I return to my car, I find that I have been hiking for five hours).

Native American rock shelter near Cartago Creek. 1995, Author's photograph.

THE SPIRIT IN THE DESERT

Perhaps you will find this meditation by the spiritual writer, Esther de Waal, *An Awareness Walk,* helpful to you as you consider a visit to this place. In it she comments on and quotes from the writing of a spiritual master whom we have already met, Thomas Merton's *New Seeds of Contemplation.*

It is only too easy to fail to see what is around us, to become unobservant, bored, unaware...Yet to see, to feel, to touch are gifts given to us to use fully and gloriously. 'Open you eyes and see'—this was something that Thomas Merton said time and again—'see directly what is in front of us.' He would go to each thing, allow it to communicate its essence, reveal what it would. This asks of us that we take time, become sensitive to the thing itself, allowing it to be what it is and to say what it wants to say. Merton respected the power of God's creation to bear witness for itself. Here is the sense that we find in poets and artists that 'the observed particulars take on the mystery of revelation.'

Merton wrote: 'It is good and praiseworthy to look at some real created thing and feel and appreciate its reality. Just let the reality of what is real sink into you...for through real things we can reach Him who is infinitely real.'

First of all walk deliberately. You are going to use all your five senses as you walk, so start by being aware of the light, the warmth of the sun, the touch of the air, the colours, clouds, light and shade. Then begin in greater details to notice patterns, shapes, contrasts and juxtapositions and how things relate.

Touch and feel, pick up stones and weigh them in the palm of your hand, find twigs and leaves and hold them gently. If it's sensible take off your shoes and start to walk barefoot.

Listen to the sound of water, birds, insects, far off sounds, nearer sounds, your own breathing. Notice the smell of flowers, herbs, earth and water. Try to stop thinking and simply be. Let everything drop away and instead try to be totally present to what is reaching you through your senses.

As you return you may feel that you must end with a thanksgiving exercise in which you list quite consciously the things that you have discovered that God has given you during the walk.

You may want to bring back something that you have particularly enjoyed and put it in the place where you pray.

So, before we return to the big busy world, stop and rest with me on this warm rock. Listen to the sound of the water flowing in the desert. Rejoice in God's wondrous grace in this place. Do you hear what I hear? Do you hear the voice calling to us? Do our hearts not stir with longing to come closer to that voice, to make a course correction and walk back on the right path?

Desert bones near Olancha. 1995, Author's photograph.

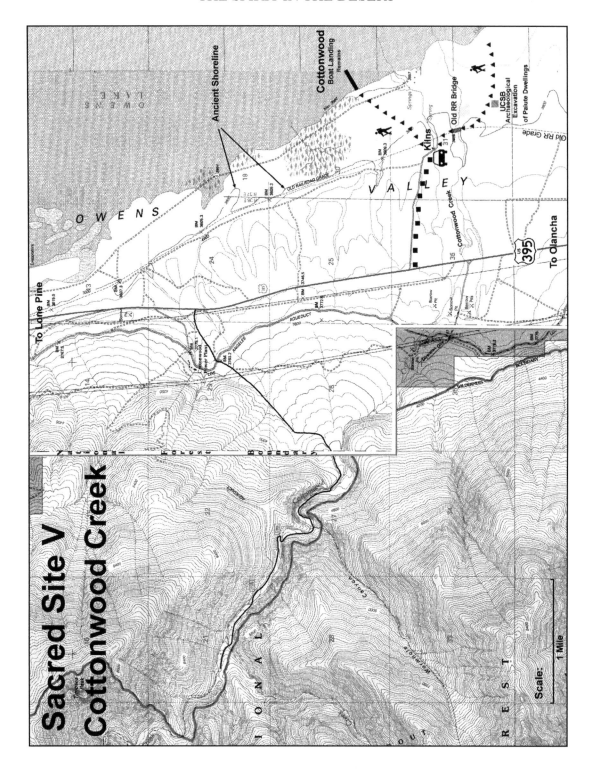

Sacred Site V
Cottonwood Creek

SACRED SITE V
COTTONWOOD CREEK

The desert has never been an end in itself. To be alone in the desert is to be alone with God. The invitation of the desert is the call to love God— absolutely.

John Moses, The Desert: An Anthology for Lent

Here is a walk through a riparian landscape and what was once the eastern shore of Owens Lake. There are two short hikes which can be made in one day.

Drive north on Highway 395 through Olancha and Cartago, the road gains elevation and becomes divided highway. Look for the directional marker to Charcoal Kilns Historic Site. Turn right onto this road and drive one mile to a parking area.

You will see the ruins of a pair of beehive-shaped charcoal kilns which are now protected by a fence. They were made of adobe brick in the latter part of the nineteenth century. A hundred and thirty years ago, a wooden flume carried cut timber from high up Cottonwood Canyon in the Sierra down to this site. The wood was cooked into charcoal in these kilns to feed the ore-refining furnaces of Cerro Gordo and Swansea. It takes some imagination to think that Owens Lake was once deep enough (between thirty and fifty feet) for two small steam ships to navigate between Swansea,

Cottonwood Creek and Cartago, busily ferrying charcoal to the furnaces and taking away huge piles of pure silver bars.

Both the walks that I propose start at the kilns. The first takes takes you over the high berm above the kilns, towards Owens Lake. As you walk through this riparian landscape, in the autumn, the trees are fiery red and orange. When you draw close to the lake, you will see the remains of the Cottonwood boat-landing. Again, fire up your imagination and think of how more than a century ago this inconsiderable pallet of planks, now half-buried in sand, was the hub of intense economic activity and daily life in this area.

The second walk will lead you up to the old Southern Pacific right-of-way, south, over the remains of a bridge which will take you across Cottonwood Creek. You can see that this is a substantial drainage channel that has carried lots of water in its history. On the south side of the creek, walk toward Owens Lake. This is a lovely walk over soft, sandy soil. If you go to the right, away from the creek bed and toward the lake, you can identify the ancient shoreline of Owens Lake.

Owens Lake was once a huge body of water, fed by glaciers and rain through the Owens River. After the lake filled, its overflow ran south past Rose Spring, through Little Lake and into Indian Wells Valley, which itself became another inland lake, and then continued to flow all the way into the parched Death Valley.

You can see a good distance as you walk. Look for a high pile of dirt and sand between the railroad bridge and the lake. You can get close to make an inspection. This is what is left of an archaeological excavation project of the University of California at Santa Barbara in which were found the remains of an ancient Paiute dwelling and evidence of daily life fifteen hundred years ago.

The best time of year to walk around Cottonwood Creek is in late fall when the colors are magnificent.

Remains of Cottonwood boat-landing, western shore of Owens Lake. 1999, Author's photograph.

Excavation of Paiute dwellings on ancient shore of Owens Lake at the mouth of Cottonwood Creek. Photograph: University of California at Santa Barbara, c.1995

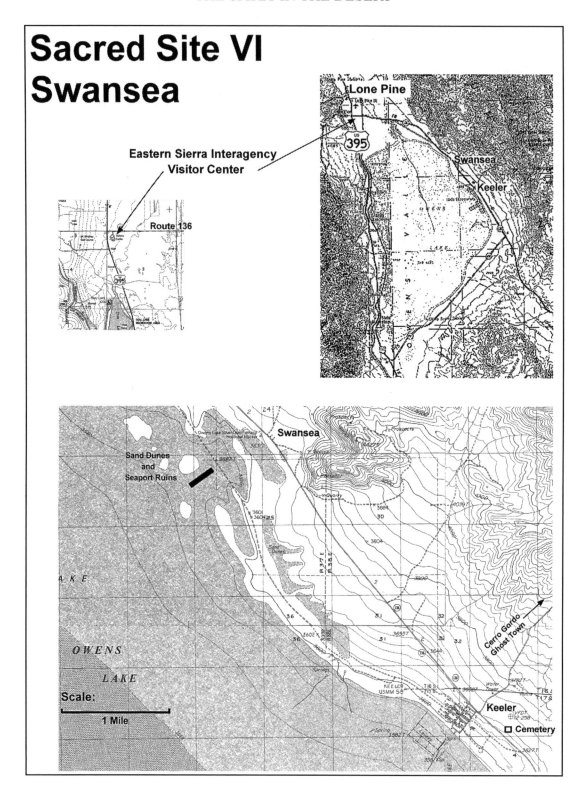

Sacred Site VI
Swansea

SACRED SITE VI
SWANSEA, KEELER AND
CERRO GORDO

You only are immortal, the creator and maker of mankind; and we are mortal, formed of the earth, and to earth we shall return. For so did you ordain when you created me, saying, 'You are dust, and to dust you shall return.' All of us go down to the dust; yet even at the grave we make our song: Alleluia, alleluia, alleluia.

Burial Office, Book of Common Prayer

This visit will take us to the lake port of Swansea, now a ghost town, to the mines of Cerro Gordo, and to some fascinating sand dunes. Along the way I will give a few general historical pointers and, as always, invite you to use the experience as the basis for contemplation.

One mile south of the town of Lone Pine, California Highway 136 heads east, leaving Highway 395, toward Death Valley. Your landmark is the Eastern Sierra Interagency Visitor Center, located at the junction of the two roads. If you stop at the Visitor Center you will find free maps and guide pamphlets and a well-stocked bookstore of desert literature. The new building provides excellent displays on Death Valley and the Owens Valley. For opening hours, the phone number is (760) 876-4252.

Take Highway 136 east. In about eleven miles you will come to the ghost port of Swansea. There is a quaint sign on the left with a few ruins of buildings from the town. The owner of the site of Swansea, whom we may meet later, also owns Cerro Gordo town site which is five thousand feet higher up, in the Inyo Mountains.

The old Wells Fargo stage station is close to the road. It is carved out of dolomite rock. You may well encounter the 'watchman' here, a noisy but friendly mule. Park your car on the right side of the road, pointing east. Close by you will see an old miner's cabin and the ruins of one of the three Cerro Gordo silver-lead smelters. There has been some significant damage to these structures due to recent flash floods. The fortunes that built Los Angeles and San Pedro Harbor came out of the ground here. Indeed, during the 1870's, mine production was so overwhelming that huge stacks of silver bars had to be piled up by the lakeshore because there were not enough teamster wagons to haul them promptly to the railroad and the cities.

One hundred and thirty years ago, Owens Lake was fifteen miles long and nine miles wide and deep enough for two steamships, decks laden with silver ingots, to keep commerce going and Swansea busy. But in 1874 a massive landslide buried the town and the owners did not have enough money to dig out and rebuild. (L. Foster describes this in his book, *Adventuring in the California Desert,* 1997).

Leave your car and walk across the highway. Watch out for the European tourists driving east to Death Valley in their rented recreational vehicles! After visiting with the mule and seeing the remaining buildings of Swansea, you are in for a treat. Walk back across the road toward the sand dunes. Can you see Mount Whitney and the Sierra Nevada in the distance? The wind can be a problem here. I always bring a bandana to cover my mouth. Walking towards the now dry lake, you pass through wonderful sand dunes. You will notice bits of charcoal scattered here and there, hinting at the silver-smelting of the past. After you pass over several dunes look for the exposed bricks which are all that remain of the seaport buildings that were buried in the landslide.

Here is a quiet, serene place to find some shelter from the wind. Sit for a little while on the sand and rest in the presence of the Lord. Here there is no time.

Security guard at Wells Fargo Stage Station, Swansea. 2000. Author's photograph.

There are more surprises when you continue walking towards the lake. If the wind is right and you have luck with erosion, the line of railroad ties from the old Southern Pacific Narrow Gauge Railroad will appear, running north and south. Until 1960, this railroad ran from Keeler to Bishop, 70 miles to the north.

You will notice the wind getting stronger as you near the lake. You will see the earth-filled remains of the old pier, where the silver ships tied up. It was in 1872 that a devastating earthquake hit this valley and the bottom of the lake, which was then filled with water, tipped up. It is hard to imagine that day.

Now, as you contemplate the quiet and beauty of these sand dunes, you will sense the price of our southern California prosperity. The Los Angeles Department of Water and Power completed its aqueduct in 1913 and began siphoning off the water from the Owens River. By 1930 the lake was virtually dry. Now, while this is one of my favorite places for desert serenity, there is danger here. When the winds are horrific, huge clouds of dry lake dust swirl up hundreds of feet into the air. When the winds blow like that, the air of this area is considered the most polluted in the United States and you will appreciate the sense of breathing through your bandana. According to the Department of the Interior, the dry lake is the largest source in the nation of PM-10, a superfine salty aerosol carrying traces of arsenic and other metals which damage lungs, machinery and crops. PM-10 from this area settles as far away as Los Angeles and the Grand Canyon. In 1975 the Navy identified the lake dust as a problem for the China Lake Naval Weapons Facility, and in 1987 the Environmental Protection Agency listed it as a source of PM-10 violations.

There was a battle between Inyo County and the City of Los Angeles over ending this form of pollution. Studies have recommended flooding some of the lake with water, and covering much of the dry lake with a mixture of gravel and salt grass. The price tag is millions of dollars, and Los Angeles, true to its historic stance, had not wanted to do the right thing. Pressed hard by little Inyo County and with the threat of loss of Federal funds, the City of Los Angeles has taken responsibility for reducing PM-10 emissions from the lake and embarked on a three-year project, so that federal clean air standard will be achieved.

If you walk out onto the lake on the land extension created by the remains of the pier, watch out for quicksand. You will be able to walk out a long way into the bed of the old lake if you stay on the higher ground.

When you return to your car, drive about three miles east to Keeler. Seventy years ago this was a bustling mining town. The ore from the silver mines was brought down to Keeler via a tramway from the mining town of Cerro Gordo, 5,000 feet above. A large talc mine provided additional work, and the town was also the southern terminus for the narrow gauge railroad which until 1938 went all the way north to Carson City, Nevada.

At the east of town, on the left side of the road is the old cemetery. It is a little hard to find, so you will have to get out of your car, walk and be watchful. The ground is very rocky here. When I last walked through here in 1997, another landslide had recently poured out of the mountains and a sudden stream of water had eroded part of the cemetery. When you find the cemetery, you will be walking through a prototypical mining town boothill. The old wooden headboards are sandblasted by desert winds and hard to read, but there are some well-preserved stone monuments.

When I walk here, I pray for the souls of the dead. As I feel the dry, harsh wind and sun, I read the monuments and try to grasp the story of the person who died.

Always there are the graves of infants, children, mothers, and miners who died too young. Who walked to this place full of grief and loss, singing those old songs, behind the horse-drawn hearse and in the simplest of liturgies expressed their daily faith in God, which was part of survival and hope in this desert land?

Pioneer grave at Keeler. 1997, Author's photograph.

Now I find a comfortable place in the sand dunes, sheltered from the wind off the dry lake, to make a spiritual exercise. I begin by reading aloud from the gospels the Temptation of Jesus in the Desert. Then I invite the Lord into my presence and ask of Jesus, *I want to know more about you so that I may love you more intensely and walk with you more closely.* And so, in imagination, enter into the experience of Jesus in the desert.

Shusaku Endo, in *A Life of Jesus,* imagines that Jesus learned something new about God when he went into the desert for forty days. As Endo entered into this gospel scene with his imagination, he saw that Jesus came to experience God differently from the harsh and demanding God of John the Baptist. For Jesus, God could be called *Abba, my own dear Father.* (Barry, p. 51)

THE SPIRIT IN THE DESERT

Can you ask the Lord for the grace to know the close presence of Abba Father?

My daily life at home in Laguna Niguel can be filled with tension, as Jan and I work to achieve some semblance of normalcy with our family. I am aware that a part of me flees to the desert as a refuge from this stress and tension. Now, as part of this spiritual exercise, I open Thomas Merton's seminal book, *Thoughts in Solitude*, (1958). This passage reminds me of the spiritual tension we encounter in the desert.

The Desert Fathers believed that the wilderness had been created as supremely valuable in the eyes of God precisely because it had no value to men. The wasteland was the land that could never be wasted by men because it offered them nothing. There was nothing to attract them. There was nothing to exploit. The desert was the region in which the Chosen People had wandered for forty years, cared for by God alone. They could have reached the Promised Land in a few months if they traveled directly to it. God's plan was that they should learn to love Him in the wilderness and that they should always look back upon the time in the desert as the idyllic time of their life with Him alone.

The desert was created simply to be itself, not to be transformed by men into something else. So too the mountain and the sea. The desert is therefore the logical dwelling place for the man who seeks to be nothing but himself—that is to say, a creature solitary and poor and dependent upon no one but God, with no great project standing between himself and his Creator.

That is, at least, the theory. But there is another factor that enters in. First, the desert is the country of madness. Second, it is the refuge of the devil, thrown out into the 'wilderness of Upper Egypt' to 'wander in dry places.' Thirst drives man mad, and the devil himself is mad with a kind of thirst for his own lost excellence—lost because he had immured himself in it and closed out everything else.

So the man who wanders into the desert to be himself must take care that he does not go mad and become the servant of the one who dwells there in a sterile paradise of emptiness and rage.

Yet look at the deserts today. What are they? The birthplace of a new and terrible creation, the testing-ground of the power by which man seeks to un-create what God has blessed. Today, in the century of man's greatest technological achievement, the wilderness at last comes into its own. Man no longer needs God, and he can live in the desert on his own resources. He can build there his fantastic, protected cities of withdrawal and experience meditation and vice. The glittering towns that spring up overnight in the desert are no longer images of the City of God, coming down from heaven to enlighten the world with the vision of Peace. They are not even replicas of the great tower of Babel that once rose up in the desert of Senaar, that man 'might make his name famous and reach even unto heaven' (Genesis 11:4). They are brilliant and sordid smiles of the devil upon the face of the wilderness, cities of secrecy, where each man spies on his brother, cities through whose veins money runs like artificial blood, and from whose womb will come the last and greatest instrument of destruction.

Can we watch the growth of these cities and not do something to purify our own hearts? When man and his money and machines move out into the desert, and dwell there, not fighting the devil as Christ did, but believing in his promises of power and wealth, and adoring his angelic wisdom, then the desert itself moves everywhere. Everywhere is desert. Everywhere is solitude in which man must do penance and fight the adversary, and purify his own heart in the grace of God.

The desert is the home of despair. And despair, now, is everywhere. Let us not think that our interior solitude consists in the acceptance of defeat. We cannot escape anything by consenting tacitly to be defeated. Despair is an abyss without bottom. Do not think to close it by consenting to it and trying to forget you have consented.

This, then, is our desert: to live facing despair, but not to consent. To trample it down under hope in the Cross. To wage war against despair unceasingly. That war is our wilderness. If we wage it courageously, we will find Christ at our side. If we cannot face it, we will never find Him.

To complete your retreat, after the desert port of Swansea and the trading town of Keeler, I hope you will take the road up the hill from Keeler to the old ghost town of Cerro Gordo (in English, Fat Hill). This legendary historic site is especially important to me and I will not forget my first visit there, but please do not visit Cerro Gordo unannounced. I usually phone a week before I intend to visit and leave a message with Mike Patterson who is the owner of the little town, giving my phone number. I do not make the trip without his okay. The phone number and address: (760) 876-5030, P. O. Box 221, Keeler, CA 93530. There is an official website: www.cerrogordo.us

Cerro Gordo is also a place where you can make an overnight retreat. Mike is open to individuals and groups who want to spend the night or weekend in one of the historic buildings. Again, you will need to make definite reservations with him.

The well-maintained dirt road begins a gentle climb past an old silver mill. I believe a standard passenger car would be able to make the trip. You will be using low gear when you come back down the hill. The season to visit is May through October, weather permitting. It takes about twenty-five minutes to make the seven-and-a-half mile trip, and as you climb higher the road narrows to the width of one car. There are several turnouts, but you will need to look ahead for any cars coming downhill. About halfway up, you will see incredible views of the Sierra Nevada and Owens Lake.

View of Cerro Gordo and Owens Lake. 2006, Author's photograph.

When you arrive, usually Mike will greet you and show you around the old general store and the wonderfully restored American Hotel, and orient you to the site. Someone has lived here continuously since the active mining of the 1800s, which is why there has been very little vandalism. You will also see a rare sight: a complete hoisting works for the biggest mine at Cerro Gordo. Mike will invite you to walk about the place and poke around the past. In appreciation you can make a donation to the Cerro Gordo Historical Society. The money goes to the preservation of this grand place.

The love of Mike's life is Jody Stewart Patterson, his wife, who died in 2001. I first met Jody in the early 1990s. She was a legendary entrepreneur and the matriarch of Swansea and Cerro Gordo. When I am on my own, I walk with the ghosts of history who are so palpable here. My favorite place for long meditation is at the cemetery, across the ravine from the town site. Jody's grave is there with an old wrought-iron bench alongside. I sit on the bench, and below me spills out the town site, a vast landscape of mining history, the backdrop is a wide-screen view of Owens Lake, 5,000 feet below. You will find that time stops here. The sounds are captivating in this beautiful place: groaning metal, swaying juniper and pinyon pine, and the moaning of creaking boards. Use your imagination to sense the dangerous struggle for life here one hundred and twenty-five years ago and the intoxicating obsession with finding silver and gold. The spirits now rest. When I sit on the bench by Jody's grave, I share this prayer for her and the six hundred others who are buried in the cemetery:

"Rest eternal grant to Jody, O Lord, and may light perpetual shine upon her. May her soul and the souls of these faithful departed rest in peace. Amen."

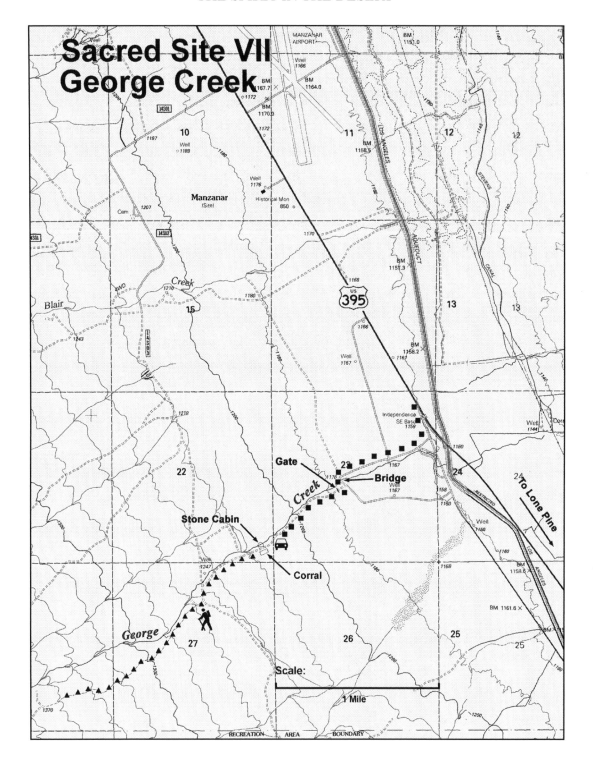

SACRED SITE VII
GEORGE CREEK
AND A STONE CABIN IN THE WOODS

To sit on rocks, to muse o'er flood and fell

To slowly trace the forest's shady scene...

This is not solitude, 'tis but to hold

Converse with Nature's charms and view her stores unrolled.

Lord Byron, Solitude

If you have only a little time and are not intending to exert yourself, here is a suggestion for a meditative walk that I have found pleasantly cool (in due season) and fruitful. An average passenger car can negotiate the route to the site.

From Lone Pine, the turn-off is an eight-minute drive north along Highway 395. It is safest to continue up the road to the Manzanar site (which we will visit in the next chapter), turn around there and go south for a right turn. Drive along the dirt road over the cattle guards and take the first road going right. This area is popular for trout fishing in the summer.

You will be heading towards the Sierra Nevada, and will find yourself running parallel to George Creek—named after a famous Owens Valley Paiute chief. This is open range, so drive carefully looking for cows and heifers. A turn-off to the left will take you over a simple bridge and the road continues west on the other side, still with the mountains ahead.

You will come to a livestock gate. The rule of the open range is: *if the gate is open, leave it open; if it is closed (and there is not a 'no trespassing sign') you can open the gate and close it behind you.* This gate will take some careful pulling as it consists of barbed wire and lumber.

You are now driving through the earliest Euroamerican settlement in the Owens Valley. The rancher and farmer John Shepherd (1833–1908) created a cattle ranch right here beside George Creek in 1862.

Keep your eyes open for an old corral on the left and a thick grove of trees on the right. When you arrive at the corral, pull your car off the road. Walk to the thick grove of trees on the right. You will be walking towards George Creek. Because you will be in this area when the weather is cooler, I hope, the trees will be barren and you will be able to spot the old stone cabin. As you walk toward it, begin to imagine the Shepherd family and their life here. Note the fine craftsmanship that went into building the solid stone walls and the engineering and physics that combined to create the door and windows. The walls are still over eight feet high. Here is a quiet place to meditate, with the comforting sounds of rushing water and the wind blowing through the aspen and cottonwood trees. When you cross the road towards the corral, you can walk around and guess where the barn would have been.

In the winter of 2002 I walked on the road past the cabin, west towards the Sierra. The temperature was 38°F at nine in the morning. I was close to the creek which was frozen solid with ice. As the sun climbed higher, the warm rays illumined the ice and I could hear the continuous crack of nature's defrosting. By eleven-thirty the temperature was 55°F. This is a land of dramatic changes. I continued walking the road and sipping water. The mountains ahead were covered with new snow. The walking rhythm of body and breath and the dramatic awakening of the earth gave me a joyful awareness of the present moment.

In his article, 'Ultimate Sanctum' for the Jesuit journal, *America,* (April 2001), Thomas J. McCarthy shares his experience of the Spirit in the desert. What he has to say corresponds well with the productive solitary mood that the Shepherd's cabin and George Creek evoke, and I can do no better than quote it at length here.

Desert is wilderness...desolate, hostile terrain that defies but does not preclude life. As I pass dutifully from yet another Lent into yet another Easter, I can't help asking what it is in me that seeks and find the richness of the desert...as metaphor, as landscape, as soulscape. The desert has long been rich soil for ascetic seclusion among anchorites, monks, even Christ himself, not to mention those raised to emulate such holiness. But if I weren't Christian, if I espoused no organized relig0ion, would the wild and unforgiving desert still move me to peer over the precipice as it does?

To answer, I turn to a favorite desert classic, Edward Abbey's *Desert Solitaire.* For Abbey the desert is a place to be alone but not lonely: 'Loneliness has passed like a shadow, has come and is gone.' What transforms the ache of loneliness into the solace of solitude is for Abbey as simple and as elusive as attention to detail. Stripped nearly bare, the landscape unveils itself with the clarity of 'sparseness and simplicity so that the living organism stands out bold and brave and vivid against the lifeless sand a barren rock.'

The desert is, for Abbey as for the Lenten sojourner, the ultimate sanctum. In removing us from the world, it draws us out of ourselves even while forcing us into our own deepest regions. 'Wilderness, wilderness.' The word suggests the past and the unknown, the womb of earth from which we all emerged.

This is how the desert, wilderness, is so intertwined in the human story: we wander in places inhospitable to life seeking answers to questions we haven't yet articulated. The desert, like the human endeavor, is layered in dust and mystery, a life process now withering, now rejuvenating that shows no sign of ceasing.

As I age and go about exploring the desert wilderness, it seems that any attempt to separate in my mind the desert as metaphor from the literal desert becomes impossible. To be parched and want water; to feel the relentless heat and want shade; to cry out and hear no echo: such are the sets of yearning to which we aspire and that we dread as human beings and broken believers. How can we know God unless we've been radically alone, deserted?

If we go (to the desert), we will know something of the desert's emptiness; and such emptiness, I have to believe, is its own reward.

At mid-day I take a lunch break within a grove of cottonwood trees beside George Creek. As I watch the water rushing over rocks and pooling behind a natural dam in front of me, I notice the trees reflected in the water. It seems that the Jesuits have a penchant for the sort of spirituality that attaches to such a setting, and also writing in *America* (April 1998), Martha Cadena tells of a similar experience beside a creek:

> I realized that the trees above me were being reflected on the surface of the water. I was struck by the insight that God is very much like the trees overhead. In this life a person cannot 'look up' and see God directly; one can only see God reflected through creation, as the trees were reflected for me in the stream. But unless one is able to be quiet and attentive during times of prayer, it is easy to miss the presence of God entirely.

Janice and Erik, Stone Cabin Ruins, 2003. Author's collection.

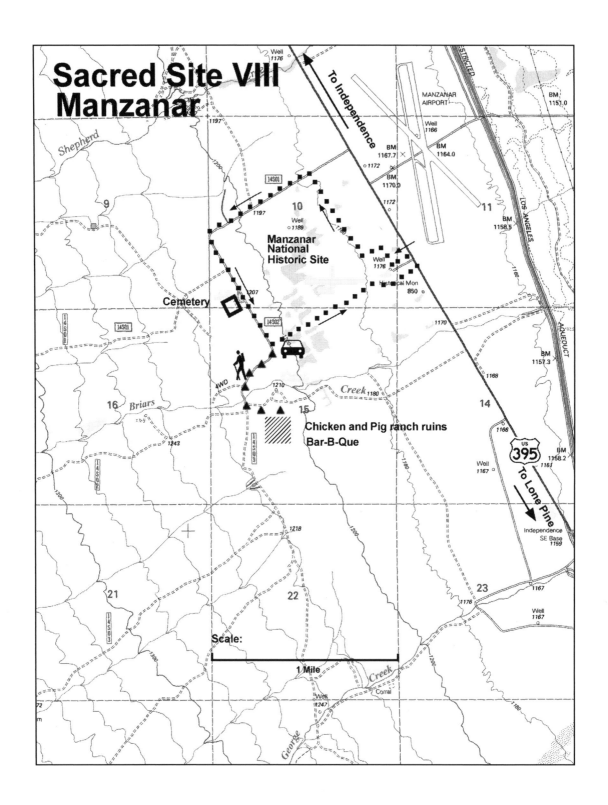

Sacred Site VIII
Manzanar

Manzanar National Historic Site

Cemetery

Chicken and Pig ranch ruins
Bar-B-Que

To Independence

To Lone Pine

Scale:

1 Mile

SACRED SITE VIII
MANZANAR RELOCATION CAMP

Pursuant to the provisions of Civilian Exclusion Order No. 33, this Headquarters, dated May 3, 1942, all persons of Japanese ancestry, both alien and non-alien, will be evacuated...by 12 o'clock noon, P.W.T., Saturday May 9, 1942.

J. L. DeWitt, Lieut. General, U.S. Army

The entrance to Manzanar Relocation Camp is less than nine miles north of Lone Pine. Look for the flagstone sentry towers on the west side of Highway 395.

Koki A. was my friend through two years of high school in Pasadena, California. We both had been elected to the executive board of the California-Nevada-Hawaii District of the Key Club, a high school boys' service organization. Koki was the Treasurer and I was the Governor. We were high school big-shots together, visiting other Key Clubs to promote service projects and so on.

Once, in 1962, I made an after-dinner speech at San Marino High School with the bread-and-butter talk I had given dozens of times. The climax of the speech was an emotional narrative about the life of Sandy Ninnenger, a World War II hero who also had been a Key Clubber. I described his heroic assault of a Japanese machine-gun nest, how he killed single-handed more than a dozen Japanese, for which act he won the Congressional Medal of Honor. Ninnenger was a paragon of the virtues of the Key Club.

As we walked to the car after the meeting Koki was stone-cold silent and he said nothing during the drive home. The next day at school I asked Koki why he was upset. He looked me straight in the eye. I can still feel the penetrating gaze through his thick eyeglasses, and his seething anger. As far as I recall, these were his words: "I resent the story you told last night. I was born at the relocation camp in Manzanar. Whenever I hear stories like that, about 'killing all those Japs,' I remember that I am Japanese. I remember how my parents lost their home and their business, and had to live in a concentration camp in the desert. They were American citizens!"

My first response was to say, "You shouldn't feel like that. You're being over-sensitive. My parents were both Navy vets of that war." Our relationship faded into the distance after that day. As I now recall his face and the depth of his feelings, I am embarrassed at my unconscious naiveté and insensitivity.

In March 1998 I made a visit to the site of Manzanar and made it the base of my Lenten desert retreat.

During the short trip north on Highway 395, I recall another journey that I made in 1980 to another concentration camp. I remember driving a rented Dutch Mitsubishi Colt through Checkpoint Charlie in divided Berlin, and south to Weimar, East Germany. At a bend in the road through a lovely forest was the entrance to a Soviet army base. Five miles further I came upon the ruins of Buchenwald. It was a gray, drizzly day. I remember the sites of the guard towers, electrified fences and the crematorium built by the same German company which efficiently constructed the ovens of Auschwitz. Next to the crematorium was the building where horrific medical experiments were done.

Just eight miles from Weimar, one of the golden cities of the European Enlightenment, where Goethe, Schiller and Bach were shining stars of German cultural achievement, Buchenwald is a testimony to human suffering.

There seems to be an age demarcation among Germans. If I ask a German over the age of seventy, "Didn't you know about these concentration camps and the killings?" the typical response is, "We did not know about all of this. How terrible!" Those below that age in West Germany have been required to process the Holocaust in their public school education. A student of mine at Saddleback College and former resident of East Germany participated in school study trips to Buchenwald.

And now I come to Manzanar.

Just outside the perimeter fence that surrounded Manzanar stood eight guard towers—one at each corner of the camp, and four positioned at points mid-way between the corner towers. Each tower stood 50 feet tall; they were topped by an enclosed guard station, with a searchlight mounted on the roof.

These towers were the main surveillance points from which armed U. S. Army Military Police kept an eye on the Manzanar population. The M.P.'s also manned the stone house at the main gate that was closest to the highway—anyone entering or leaving Manzanar had to clear this checkpoint.

The M.P. detachment at Manzanar was equipped, in 1942, with 21 rifles, 89 shotguns, 6 machine guns, and 21 submachine guns. The M.P.'s were authorized to shoot to kill if anyone attempted to break through the fence.

The Manzanar Committee, *Self-Guided Tours of Manzanar*

Today, a bronze plaque at the main gate proclaims that Manzanar is a National Historic Site. Only ten feet away, another memorial plaque proclaims that this section of Highway 395 is a memorial to those who heroically gave their lives for the defense of their country in World War II. The two plaques seem to face each other in angry confrontation: "Manzanar was a concentration camp!" or "Manzanar was for the good and safety of Japanese non-citizens, who could have been harmed, or could have harmed our country during a time of war!" Just as in Germany, in the Owens Valley there appears an age demarcation when the subject of Manzanar comes up. Those over seventy tend to see the camp as for the protection of Japanese Americans. Those under seventy tend to hold the image of a concentration camp.

Manzanar was designated a National Historic Site by Congress in 1992. In the area near the old camp community building, heavy equipment has been renovating the campsite. Superintendent Ross Hopkins presented a master plan that entails reconstructing some of the camp's grounds and buildings, provide interpretative tours, and restoring the auditorium, the only surviving building in the camp, as a visitor's center and museum (Cf. *The New York Times,* June 20, 1998).

Manzanar has been home to three distinct heritages: the Northern Paiute, the European-American farmers, and the Japanese-American prisoners. For a thousand years, family groups of migrating Northern Paiute lived along the banks of Briar Creek, which now delineates the southern boundary of the relocation camp. The Native Americans were driven out by white settlers in 1863. Extensive archaeological excavations have unearthed evidence of long-time native occupation. Numerous grinding rocks, tools, campfires and rock shelter sites have been identified. (Cf. Proceedings of the Fourth Death Valley Conference on History and Prehistory, p. 193).

As you walk the bone-dry, sandy paths, it is difficult to imagine the farming community that flourished here in the early 1900s. Manzanar means 'Apple Orchard,' and the success of the farms was largely because of the abundant water flowing from the Sierra snow melt. But this water was absorbed into the Aqueduct system after the City of Los Angeles bought up most of the land in the valley in the 1920s. Ideal farmland became desert waste.

To orient myself to the relocation camp, I drive past the sentry gate, and take the main camp road, which runs north and south, past the old community center. A maze of roads extends from the main road in a complex grid pattern. In some spots the sand is deep, and without front-wheel drive I would have become stuck.

Barbeque at the Manzanar Chicken Ranch. Author photograph, 2000

Children and Young Adults at Manzanar. Photograph: Dorothea Lange, National Archives.

To begin exploration of the camp on foot, I park at the southern boundary, close to Briar Creek. Although it is late March, the cold, moist breath of El Niño gusts across California. The thermometer shows 38°F. Snow is falling in the distance, like sifting powdered sugar. I pull my Stetson down tight over my head, button the jacket up to the neck, and begin to walk west towards the Sierra on an old camp road running parallel to the creek and now roaring with snow-melt. The formerly enclosed city of ten thousand souls is littered with ruins of rock walls, concrete foundation pads, piles of metal barrel hoops, and a broken line of the unique irrigation system leading back to Briar Creek. Where sagebrush and wildflowers now grow, according to the map, there were once buildings tightly-packed together.

The brush is dense, but I have learned to follow deer and cattle trails to find a way through this kind of undergrowth. A trail leads me to the banks of the creek and a crossing point where they narrow. With a leap of faith I jump the cold, swift waters. I climb the red-clay bank on the other side and find that I have arrived in another world. Before me, spilled out across several acres, are more ruins: concrete building pads and rock-decorated paths. At the center is the largest barbeque I have ever seen.

These are the ruins of the chicken and pig ranch, which the Japanese-American inmates developed as a food and income source. As I draw close to the over-sized brick-and-stone barbeque, I imagine a summer Sunday afternoon, the smell of mesquite wood, teriyaki sauce and cooking chicken and ribs. I can see entire families gathering here, pretending they are free, at home, back in normal life.

The wind howls through the cottonwood trees. My hands are ice-cold. I put on gloves, pull the kerchief across my lips and nose, and walk back to the creek crossing.

On the other side I walk north along a barbed-wire fence. A thick forest of cottonwood and old fruit trees is on my right and I turn toward them. Maybe I can escape the wind if I go into the old orchard. I imagine the farmers and their apples and pears, the vivid colors of healthy fruit trees flowering in late spring and irrigated by the abundant water. Then I imagine the Japanese-American inmates pruning these trees in the cold winter wind. The forest is now thick with neglected old branches and in the tallest tree I clearly see the bundled twigs of a golden eagle's abandoned nest. That bird flew free over the internment camp.

I have lost sense of time again. How long have I been walking? I am deep within the orchard where the wind cannot get to me but I can hear its sustained, sad cry howling through the treetops. The dusting of snow is coming much closer.

Through the trees, toward the mountains, I see the white stone monument of the Japanese-American cemetery. I sit on a log and focus on the obelisk. Visitors have left small stones on the grave markers with a few sake cups. An offering of toys marks a child's grave. My mind flashes back to the time when I was born. I imagine Koki as a baby, held in his mother's arms. I see his older sister and father as they huddle before a tiny stove in their small house here in the camp. The same sighing, cold wind blows upon them. In the summer the heat would blister the paint off the wooden walls and the fine sand would persistently penetrate the walls and windows of the buildings.

I sit in the shelter of this abandoned orchard of forgotten fruit. The water and the people are gone. The desert wind sounds like the beckoning call of ancestor spirits who are now also forgotten and wandering as hungry ghosts. When people were here, the Shinto rituals remembered the souls by name and fed them. No one is here now to remember the dead. But in April each year the children and grandchildren of the inmates return to Manzanar for a prayer service of remembrance. And, for the last few years members of the Paiute-Shoshone, who live on the reservations in Lone Pine and Big Pine, have joined this memorial service.

After you have visited the camp, you will want to travel fifteen minutes north on Highway 395 to the little town of Independence which hosts the Eastern California Museum. Here there is a research library where there is an extensive display about the three heritages of Manzanar. It clearly shows the resilience of the human spirit despite barbed wire and machine guns and guard towers. For instance, the display illustrates how some inmates who were forced to leave jobs as schoolteachers formed the Manzanar camp school which became one of the finest school districts in California during the war years.

But it was an evil spirit that inspired the creation of the concentration camp at Manzanar and that same spirit continues to feed and inspire revisionist history and denial today. How can healing and wholeness come to this valley, unless at least some confession can be expressed: "What a terrible thing was done to these brothers and sisters"? As war was the context for all sorts of twisted thinking that justified Buchenwald, what similar justifications still move in the minds of many people, some of whom yet live close by in this valley?

Where is Jesus walking at Manzanar? And what is his conversation with the evil and pain that still lives here? Father Claude Nicolas, who, as the exorcist at the Notre Dame Cathedral in Paris, was quoted in the *New York Times* (June 15, 1998) on the existence of evil. He said: "Yes. I believe the Devil exists, but not in the way he is popularly presented. The evil spirit exists in people's hearts. It slips in through the mind's fault lines. It destroys trust, causes despair, prevents people from loving, from living a full life."

Jesus, we want to walk closely beside you here at Manzanar.

We can read the healing-exorcism stories in the Gospel of Mark 9:14-29, and 5:1-20 and consider what it was like for Jesus to face those who were possessed by demons. As I walk with Jesus on these sandy, desert trails of Manzanar, I ask him to help me and everyone who is redeemed, to be unafraid before the power of evil. I ask Jesus to give us the courage to stand against evil as we place ourselves within the protective circle of God's love.

We read the gospel stories to seek more knowledge of Jesus. We see that he accepts life as a struggle between good and evil rather than debating the philosophical existence of evil—along the lines of, 'If God is all-loving, all-powerful and all-knowing, why does God allow suffering?' Whether it is through Buchenwald or Manzanar that we walk, we find our rational mind struck cold by the stark reality of evil. In his book (Ave Maria Press, 1996) *Who Do You Say I Am?* the theologian William Barry shares:

> One of the odd things is that we spend a good deal of time discussing the origin of evil, but we spend less time working out practical methods of tackling the problem... Jesus saw the essential struggle between good and evil, which is at the heart of life and raging in the world. He did not speculate about it; he dealt with it and gave to others the power to overcome evil and do the right. We might want to ask Jesus for help to have his attitude in the face of evil and thus be freed of wasting time and energy speculating about the origins of evil.

But debate and posturing and parsing of words continues in the case of the evil that was Manzanar Relocation Camp, which was itself, of course, part of the greater evil called war. Here are a few paragraphs from four different sources to take away with you after your visit to Manzanar. The first is from W. Hastings of the town of Bishop, Letters to the Editor, *The Inyo Register,* May 7, 1998.

> Manzanar: Another, Different Look
>
> Guard towers did not exist at Manzanar. But a couple of fire watch towers... The towers had searchlights at the tops so that the Japanese interior police force could follow persons walking within Manzanar at night, thereby helping to reduce robberies and beatings at night.
>
> The words 'forcibly relocated to Manzanar' ...is just a play on words. President Roosevelt built and made available to those that wished to move to the camps. They were not required to move to these camps.

And from the January 15, 1998 issue of the *Inyo Register,* below is a letter from Richard White, Chairman of the Friends of the Eastern California Museum, Independence, CA.

> Manzanar was one of ten WWII camps built by the federal government to house Japanese Americans during WWII... Once the Wartime Civil Control Administration took control of the camps, they established an

103

official terminology: the camps were to be called 'Relocation Camps', and the residents of the camps to be called 'Evacuees'. Those removed to the camps were also termed 'alien' or 'non-alien'—another term for American Citizen. However, not everyone in the federal government used the official WRA terminology. Those who used the term 'concentration camp' when describing Manzanar included Presidents Roosevelt and Truman, the Attorney General, Supreme Court Justices, the Secretary of the Interior and the Secretary of War.

The National Park Service will not use that term to refer to the Manzanar National Historic Site.

However, (Manzanar) is about larger questions—what can (and will) our nation do to our own residents and citizens during a time of war, national emergency, or perceived national emergency? What individual or collective rights are we, as citizens, guaranteed in this great nation?

I strongly believe that placing more than 115,000 people in camps during WWII for the primary reason of skin color and racial heritage is wrong— no matter what terminology we use in describing the camps. Identifying American Citizens of Japanese ancestry with the Japanese enemy was a mistake. I am proud that America is a place where mistakes can be recognized and acknowledged, and that we as a nation can learn from our mistakes in order that they are not repeated.

In 1980, the United States Congress established the Commission on Wartime Relocation and Internment of Civilians, which made this final report:

The broad historical causes which shaped these decisions were race prejudice, war hysteria and a failure of political leadership... A grave injustice was done to American citizens and resident aliens of Japanese ancestry who, without individual review or any probative evidence against them, were excluded, removed and detained by the United States during WWII.

Our governments have offered an official apology and reparations to those who were placed in Manzanar and camps like it. The President and the state of California signed the apology letters sent to each survivor:

A monetary sum and words alone cannot restore lost years or erase painful memories; neither can they fully convey our Nation's resolve to rectify injustice and to uphold the rights of individuals. We can never fully right the wrongs of the past. But we can take a clear stand for justice and recognize that serious injustices were done to Japanese Americans during WWII.

I have not seen Koki A. since 1963. Perhaps we will see each other at a high school reunion. What will we say to each other?

Manzanar Roman Catholic Church. Photograph: Ansel Adams, Library of Congress,

The Manzanar National Historic Site is located on the west side of Highway 395, nine miles north of Lone Pine and six miles south of Independence.

When you visit Manzanar you will learn about the experiences of Japanese Americans as well as about the earlier inhabitants of the area. You can drive a 3.2 mile auto tour and see remnants of orchards, rock gardens, building foundations and the camp cemetery. The Interpretive Center offers extensive exhibits, a short film and an excellent bookstore. www.nps.gov/manz

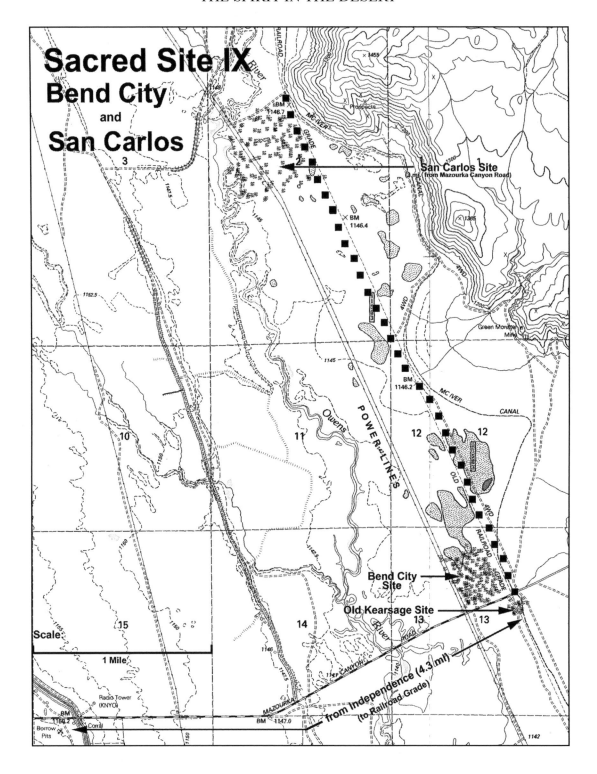

SACRED SITE IX
BEND CITY AND SAN CARLOS

We camped on the river near Bend City… It is a miserable hole of perhaps twenty-five adobe houses built on the sand in the midst of the sagebrush, but there is a large city laid out –on paper. It was intensely hot, there appeared to be nothing done, times dull…

Journal of Geologist William H. Brewer, 1864

I first read of these two desert towns in William Chalfant's classic account, *The Story of Inyo.* Chalfant was one of the great newspapermen of the Old West. He vividly describes the daily life and vitality of the pioneer towns in the center of the Owens Valley in the 1860s. Those were turbulent times, when the Shoshone-Paiute controlled most of the access to the area. After several violent skirmishes between the indigenous people and the new settlers, a US Army outpost fort was built at Independence. This allowed Bend City and San Carlos to develop in some milieu of safety and stability for a brief period.

Over several years I researched maps trying to locate precisely these two pioneer towns. I could not match the coordinates of old maps to new roads and highways. Recent books about Owens Valley gave conflicting information, but eventually I had enough to go on.

I drove north on Highway 395 to Independence. At Mazourka Canyon Road, just before entering town, there is an auto-repair shop built of native stone on the east side of the road. I turned east towards the Inyo Mountains and went about three miles until the end of the pavement. A dirt road continues climbing east into Mazourka Canyon. Another dirt road, which turns out to be the bed of the old Southern Pacific narrow-gauge railroad, intersects at this point. On the south side of this intersection is the site of the railroad station-settlement of Kearsarge. I parked my car, and began to walk the area between the power lines and the right-of-way of the old railroad, north of Mazourka Road. My guess was that the site of Bend City must be here.

This is a beautiful and quiet place to walk and look for history. The landscape is broad and expansive, filled with desert brush and some cottonwoods by the river. To the west, the magnificent Sierra Nevada.

I walked north and found the outlines of stone buildings, a granite-slab threshold, and hillocks of slag from the smelting of precious metals. Here and there the sagebrush grew on large earth mounds. As I looked carefully into the sagebrush I could see faintly the remains of adobe walls. I walked further north and then west. The outlines of the dwellings became clearer and within an area of several acres I could identify twenty adobe ruins, each with outlines of stone, among which there was a scattering of square, hand-forged nails.

I came to a large depression, which looked like the course of an old river. Indeed, this had been the Owens River which had given life to this little town. Back when there was water, the several diversion channels must have made the place look like a little Amsterdam. Unfortunately, one early morning in 1872 Mother Nature struck with a vengeance. The most powerful earthquake in California history devastated the Owens Valley, most of the adobe buildings hereabouts collapsed, and the Owens River changed its course.

Where was the sister town of San Carlos? I returned to my car and began to follow some vague clues from maps and other guides. From where the pavement ends I turned north and drove carefully over a hard-clay surface. In some places flashfloods had eroded the road. Again, this is open rangeland, and in spring and fall, protective cows are out here with their calves—they are all over the place. I drove three miles north on the old roadbed. The Inyo Mountains are close to this road. When there was enough space I pulled over and parked.

I looked to the west and could now see extensive brick foundations of the town of the 1860s. Apparently, San Carlos had been a much more developed town than Bend City, boasting hotels, restaurants, a newspaper office, the Wells Fargo station, and all the little stores and shops necessary to support the life of pioneer settlers in the middle of the desert. Walking around with a careful eye, I found hard-rock mineshafts in the hillside and a well.

When I first visited here, the old post-earthquake riverbed was dramatically empty. Stark, brittle-barked, dead trees and salt grass lined its banks. But, imagining the time when water flowed in the river, I could see the vital and active city of San Carlos.

The other desert towns of the Owens Valley that were founded in the latter part of the 1800's owe their existence to Bend City and San Carlos. It was the life of these two towns and the gold and silver strikes in the Inyo range that drew the settlers over Montgomery Pass from Nevada.

As you walk through the ruins of Bend City and San Carlos, imagine the people who journeyed here and carved a life in these desert places, facing the real threat of sudden death, fear, loneliness and isolation. Once again, withdrawal of water, the source of life, ended those hopes

David Wright, 'The End of the Road', *The Album,* Summer, 1994

As I walk through the ruins of these two towns that were once vital with industry and optimistic about the future, I consider my own city of ministry, Santa Ana, 250 miles to the south. Founded in the 1880s by William Spurgeon during a California land-boom promoted by the Santa Fe Railroad, Santa Ana began as a village serving the great ranches of Orange County: Irvine Ranch, El Toro Ranch and Rancho Mission Viejo. With the arrival of the railroad, the town boomed and became an affluent business and residential center. World War II brought the El Toro Marine Base, and many veterans stayed after the war, buying the pleasant and affordable new tract homes, and Orange County grew and grew, with Santa Ana as its county seat.

When I walk the streets of my church's neighborhood, I can admire the renovated Victorian mansions of French Park. After a hundred and thirty years, Santa Ana has a significant population of recent immigrants and the highest proportion of native

Spanish speakers of any city in the United States. In previous decades, the churches were esteemed as centers of spiritual values, nurturing and caring for the people of Santa Ana. Nowadays the churches are seen by many city officials as institutions which, while not contributing to the tax rolls, are simply sources of traffic and parking problems. Nonetheless, congregations like the Episcopal Church of the Messiah and St. Joseph's Roman Catholic Church are vital and alive, supporting ministries to the poor, children and youth, and the immigrants: spiritual lighthouses to those in need.

My thoughts return to San Carlos and Bend City and how in 2006 a miraculous change came to this area beside a dead river. Following a court challenge brought by Inyo County, the City of Los Angeles agreed to release water from the Los Angeles Aqueduct into the Lower Owens River, to flow more than seventy miles south towards the Owens Lake. A pump station before the lake returns the water into the Aqueduct.

This is a remarkable blessing. After more than eighty years, during which the lower Owens River had become the dry riverbed choked with salt grass that I describe above, as of March 2006, the river began to flow through the old depressions near San Carlos and Bend City. So now, at San Carlos, you can find the very dusty, dirt road heading west to the Sierra which will take you to the renewed Owens River. Every day new life is returning—including abundant bass and trout. In a few years, walking the river banks by San Carlos will be a pleasant experience, the cottonwood and willow trees will grow again to shelter you from wind and sun.

The Owens River flows again after eighty years. Near San Carlos, 2007. Author's Photograph.

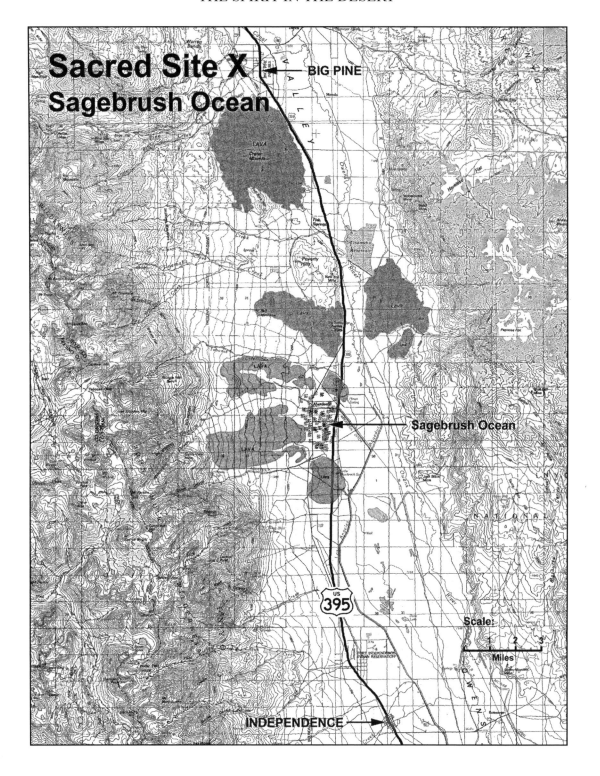

Sacred Site X
Sagebrush Ocean

BIG PINE

Sagebrush Ocean

US 395

Scale:

Miles

INDEPENDENCE

SACRED SITE X
SAGEBRUSH OCEAN

And the angel of the Lord appeared to him in a flame of fire out of the midst of a bush : and he looked, and behold, the bush burned with fire, and the bush was not consumed. ...And the Lord said, put off thy shoes from off thy feet, for the place whereon thou standest is holy ground

Exodus 3:2,5

It is November, 2004. I am driving north on Highway 395, past the flourishing little town of Independence, with its famous courthouse facing the highway. The sun has risen above the Inyos to the east, giving a rose-orange tint to a vast ocean of sagebrush opening to my right and left. There are no fences. Stopping by the side of the highway, I leave the car and walk east into this wondrous space—a sea of sage. As the sand crunches under my feet, I feel that I am on holy ground. I sense cold air, a slight wind, rising sun, swaying branches of sagebrush. A large bush in front of me is on fire, reflecting sunlight in the crisp morning air. I remember Moses on Mt. Sinai and God speaking to him in a burning bush.

I used to confuse rabbit brush and sagebrush. Look for the three-pronged silver leaves of *artemisia tridentata* or Great Basin Sage. When you walk in this sagebrush ocean, take some of the leaves and rub them between your hands and smell.

THE SPIRIT IN THE DESERT

The Owens Valley Paiutes used sagebrush as a remedy for headaches, colds and stomach problems. My understanding is that they would breathe the fumes from burning sage or drink a tea made from its dried leaves.

In the winter, when the bushes are grey and dry, I have cut twigs of the sage and bundled them with string. Then I let them fully dry out at home. When I want to remember my walks in the sagebrush ocean, I light the end of the bundle and let it smolder and carry this desert incense through the rooms of my house or my office at the church.

Several years ago after a winter walk in the desert, it came into my head to plant a small sagebrush in my home garden in Laguna Niguel, a quite different environment, five miles from the ocean. Though I watered it carefully it died, and so began my education about desert plants. I learned that water has to drain quickly in loose, desert-like soil, or the roots will rot. On my next visit to the garden supply center, I bought some packaged soil for desert plants. A few months later, I brought home another small sagebrush and planted it carefully in the artificial desert soil. The silver leaves began to appear and after a month, even though it was winter, bright yellow flowers appeared. Now, when I tend my desert guest, I feel close again to the landscape that I love.

But be aware that it is unlawful and unwise to remove desert plants from public lands such as those administered by the Bureau of Land Management or the National Forest Service. If you want to explore bringing the desert plants to your home, there are some internet resources: http://davesgarden.com and http://laspilitas.com —both provide a vast collection of information about desert plants and where you can buy them.

Whatever the season, the smell of the living desert for me is the fragrance of sagebrush. After a brief rain, a damp, sweet smell fills my senses. In the heat of summer, especially at sunset, an explosion of sage scent is perfume in the heavy, hot air of the Owens Valley.

Great Basin Sage (artemisia tridentate), 2007, author's photograph.

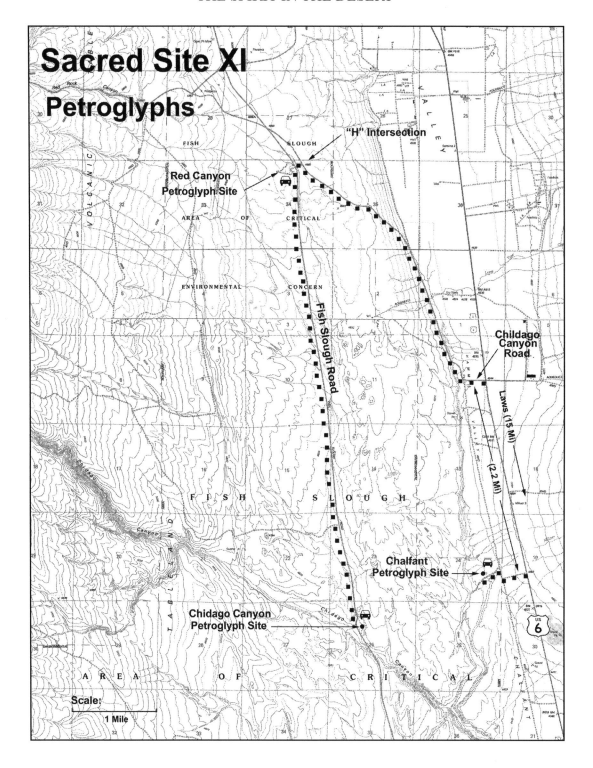

SACRED SITE XI
PETROGLYPHS OF THE
VOLCANIC TABLELANDS

It has its wild and demonic forms and can sink into an almost grisly horror and shuddering. It has its crude, barbaric antecedents and early manifestations, and again it may be developed into something beautiful and pure and glorious. It may become the hushed, trembling, and speechless humility of the creature in the presence of—whom or what? In the presence of that which is a mystery inexpressible and above all creatures.

Rudolf Otto, The Idea of the Holy

There is an area known as the Volcanic Tablelands north of the town of Bishop, between highways 6 and 395, and near the resort town of Mammoth. Over the last few years there has been a fair amount of seismic and pre-volcanic activity here. It is home to some of the finest petroglyphs in the United States.

Petroglyphs are distinguished from pictographs in that petroglyphs are chipped with a hard stone into the dark surface of rocks, the dark surface or varnish being the result of natural weathering. Pictographs are painted on.

Because the sacred sites described in this chapter are so culturally important and yet fragile, they are not for the casual tourist. I suggest taking the following steps in preparation for your visit.

Read the book, *A Guide to Rock Art Sites: Southern California and Southern Nevada,* by David S. Whitley (Mountain Press, Missoula, 1996). UCLA professor Whitley is one of the most respected experts on prehistoric art, and one of the few professional archaeologists who ties ethnographic data into his research. While most of the information I have read about this area states that the purpose of the petroglyphs remains mysterious, Dr. Whitley gives lots of enlightening ethnographic and neuropsychological information which teases apart the mysteries. I will return to his fascinating account when we reach the first petroglyphs.

On the day of your visit, your first stop should be at the Paiute-Shoshone Cultural Museum on West Line Street in downtown Bishop. The museum has excellent displays about Paiute culture and history and examples of petroglyphs. The museum will not provide directions to the petroglyphs in the Tablelands because vandalism has been a serious problem at the sites. However, there are now several published accounts of how to get to the petroglyphs, and, after sober consideration—given that this book hopefully fosters a reverent attitude to the sacred—I will add my own notes. There are also more detailed directions at the end of this chapter.

Your next stop is at the U.S. Forest Service office in Bishop where you will need to register as a visitor to the petroglyph area. The staff is helpful and friendly and you will receive a map and other information. However, this map will not be entirely clear. Instead, I prefer the Bureau of Land Management map that accompanies the chapter on petroglyphs from the book, *Adventuring in the California Desert: a Sierra Club Travel Guide,* by Lynne Foster (Sierra Club Books, 1997).

Before setting off, I must say that I strongly recommend walking in the volcanic tablelands between October and March, otherwise the weather may be too changeable. Contrary to my advice, I first visited the Red Canyon site in early June. The day before, the temperature had been 85°F., but on the morning of my visit it had dropped to 58°F. A sudden storm had brought the snow level down to 5,000 feet. When walking here you will also have to be watchful for snakes, cacti, sharp-edged lava rocks, steep inclines and cracks in the ground.

The most impressive petroglyphs are at the Red Canyon and Chalfant sites. The Forest Service map directs you along a good dirt road north of Bishop, to several of the sites. Red Canyon and Chalfant are toward the end of that hour-and-a-half journey. I preferred to go north on Highway 6, which eventually leads over Montgomery Pass and into the deserts of western Nevada. After about twenty miles, another good dirt road leads west from Bishop into the Tablelands.

Driving north on Highway 6, I passed through historic farming and mining settlements. Northeast of Big Pine the mountain range is called the White Mountains. South of Big Pine it is known as the Inyo Mountains. This is one of the rare areas in the Owens Valley where there seems to be enough water for farming.

I found the turn-off going west towards Red Canyon. The road was well-maintained, wide and graveled, the ground wet from morning rain. At a bend I had to brake suddenly and nearly went into the ditch to avoid a cow and her calf sunning in the middle of the road! A huge longhorn bull stood to the side, glaring right at me. I stopped and waited. After a few minutes, mother and calf sauntered off to the opposite side of the hill.

After climbing a steep grade, the road drops into Red Canyon, aptly named for the abundant red volcanic soil. I came to an intersection shaped like an 'H'. The road I was on continued north. A road from the south began to run parallel to my road, and a short connection allowed access to the road from the south. Here, immediately I saw the outcroppings of salmon-colored pumice and the Red Canyon petroglyphs. Small BLM warning signs identified the site. A level area has been set aside for parking.

The surprise and reality of the petroglyphs took my breath away. Because the sky was cloudy and a little dark, the scrapings in the rock varnish were easy to make out and to photograph. In full sunlight, you would need a polarizing filter to capture the images. The first etching I saw was the figure of an elongated man. Then I could see the head of big-horned sheep, some spirals, and more mysterious markings.

Dr. Whitley suggests that what you and I have walked into is a place for Native American shaman vision quests. The etchings on the rocks may be the 'dream notes' of the shamans to remind them of a vision quest, and also identifying marks, honoring spirit presences such as the 'water babies', who protected ancient water sources (now dry). Whitley's describes shamanism as, "a form of worship based on direct, personal interaction between the shaman (or medicine man) and the supernatural (or sacred realm and its spirits)." Shamans would be connected with the spirit world through trances or dreaming. In these states, the shaman could receive a spirit helper, sometimes with dangerous attributes, such as a grizzly bear or a rattlesnake. And once the shaman received such a spirit helper, the shaman in some sense actually became that creature. The totemic animal could be no longer hunted or eaten.

There is abundant literature about the nature and development of shamanism and the special calling that it entails. Accounts of shamanism occur throughout developed Native American cultures. To modern Westerners, the most famous shaman was Black Elk of the Oglala Sioux, who during his long life embraced Christianity while remaining a holy man of his tradition, finding each complementary to the other. He died in 1950.

Following the research into shaman culture there has arisen a certain romanticism about it among New Age religionists and other seekers. Some Native Americans even lead 'shaman workshops,' teaching methods of contact with the unseen world. These spiritual entrepreneurs are often severely criticized for sharing tribal secrets.

The spiritual vocation of the shaman might begin with an adolescent illness when hallucinations or vivid dreams would accompany a fever. Later these altered states could be revisited, induced through depriving the subject of food and water, or by intense drumming and dancing, or by taking hallucinogens. I was surprised to learn that the primary hallucinogen used by shamans in this area was very potent native tobacco.

Usually someone in the process of becoming a shaman was assisted by an established shaman who helped a young man adapt to the spirit presences that he encountered. After a long period of training, fasting and prayer, the new shaman would go to an isolated place, often at night, on a vision quest. Then the shaman would reconnect with the spirit world through a trance and receive power in the form of a vision. The Red Canyon site could be a place where shamans came at night, and what we now see as rock art are notations of the vision quest which helped them remember and reconnect with the unseen world.

"Vision quests were sought at numinous sites, believed to be inhabited by supernatural spirits and, more generally imbued with supernatural power," states Whitley. Caves, rocks and water sources were believed to be gateways to the sacred realm. Apparently, this area of the Tablelands, was one such gateway.

Whitley suggests that the morning after a vision quest, the shaman would paint or carve his visions on the rock at the site. These carvings would became part of the spiritual heritage of the shaman's people. It was very important that the shaman did not forget these visions lest he lose his spiritual potency and die. Can it also be possible that shamans would return to these numinous sites to revitalize the memory of that first trance and to renew their power? Were these rock art sites also desert retreat sites for these shamans?

At the Red Canyon site, three human figures are identified, with images of bighorn sheep, and the zigzag shapes of rattlesnakes. Most striking to me were the hand-prints and small foot-prints. The foot-prints (look for them on top of small rocks on the south side of the Red Canyon site) represent visions of the 'water baby' or 'water dwarf'—an unusually potent spirit helper—experienced as a short, long-haired male human wearing traditional Native American clothing.

> They believed he lived in springs and rivers and, like all supernatural spirits, was fond of native tobacco, a strong hallucinogen. The sighting of a Water Baby was believed to result in death—a metaphor, in fact, for entering or being in an altered state of consciousness. Most commonly the informants said a Water Baby's footprints could be seen around the springs and water holes where he resided." (Whitley, 1996)

The largest petroglyph site in this area north of Bishop is that of the Chalfant petroglyphs. As I studied the pictures spread out in this site, the motif of bisected circles stood out. Dr. Whitley identifies these bisected circles as 'vulva-form' petroglyphs.

> These symbolize a sexual association with the shamans' altered-state experiences, equating their entry into the supernatural with sexual intercourse; the sites themselves symbolize vaginas. (Ibid.)

A basic belief behind these sexual symbols of the vision quests is that the unseen supernatural world was intimately tied to the fertility of the visible, natural world. Through them and the shaman's magical powers, he could effect the success of harvests and hunts. Whitley comments further on the spiritual power of sex:

> Some hallucinogens used by Native Americans are also aphrodisiacs. Shamans used sexual intercourse as a metaphor to describe entering the spirit world. They expressed it symbolically by using an exaggeratedly phallus-shaped pestle in the ritual preparation of hallucinogens, and also by believing that 'wet dreams' among non-shamans in their normal sleep were the result of dangerous sexual intercourse with spirits. (Ibid.)

Such potency could be used for good or ill; it was inherently dangerous. According to Whitley, research has shown that shamans were men of great appetites whose predatory nature was widely recorded.

Young girls were warned to avoid the sexually rapacious shamans whenever possible because they might concede to the shamans' advances to avoid supernatural retribution directed to them and their family. Shamans throughout the Far West were both feared and respected, reflecting a fundamental Native American belief about supernatural power: it was inherently amoral and ambivalent, and thus could be used for good or bad. This made power dangerous to those lacking the training and ability to use it, and since the shaman was a man of power, he was necessarily a dangerous individual. Following the same logic, any inherently dangerous creature—such as rattlesnakes, grizzlies, and spiders—were also supernaturally powerful and was therefore intimately associated with shamans. The symbols of shamans were likewise potentially dangerous because of their material spirituality connecting them to the sacred. (Ibid.)

Chalfant petroglyph. Photograph: Janice Karelius, 2007.

On one rock at the Chalfant site, I found a human handprint. I placed my own within its outline –a perfect fit. I imagined that the hand was a self-portrait of a shaman after a vision quest perhaps a thousand years ago. I held my hand for a while to this connection across time.

Given that as I stand before these petroglyphs I am in a place of spiritual power and that I recognize a connection, perhaps an affinity, between it and myself, there arose in me many questions: What or whom did you meet when you entered this place? What did you seek? There are various spirits that could make their presence known; what spirits did you choose? And how did you choose among these spirits? In answer came a fundamental credo: I believe that the spirit movements of joy, peace, love and hope, self-giving love for others, care for the neighbor and those who have less or are in need, are all spiritual movements coming ultimately from the one Holy One. At the same time I believe that there are other spirits which draw us toward taking power for use against others, to oppress and threaten for selfish gain –which I do not choose.

I am seated on the highest elevated point of volcanic tufa at the Red Canyon site. I am alone and can turn to any point of the compass and see for miles. There is no sign of civilization. I am thinking about the shamans who came here seeking to enter the portals of the unseen world, and ultimately to become conduits of spiritual power within the natural world and within the tribe. And I am thinking about what their quest means for me, a human being who is a priest.

All religions describe some expression of the hunger for communion with the unseen world. So much so that it is likely that this hunger is fundamentally human. In this connection I was very interested to read the Jesuit scholar of the Zen-Christian dialogue, Father William Johnston, in his book, *Silent Music: The Science of Meditation*, (1997, Fordham University Press).

> The transition from the rational, wordy consciousness to a deeper mystical and intuitive consciousness has been the object of considerable psychological study in recent times. What precisely happens in the process of passing from an excited state characterized by beta to a relaxed awareness in which alpha predominates? One of the more widely accepted explanations is the so-called filter theory (Naranjo, pp. 170ff.). According to this, the brain, and nervous system are fitted with restrictive filters or barriers of some kind, which prevent total reality from entering consciousness, only permitting the entrance of such knowledge as man needs for biological survival. These filters are nothing less than a

repressive mechanism calculated to impede the inrush of knowledge that would otherwise overwhelm and break us. In this sense they are a sort of protective screen: humankind, unable to bear too much reality, must find some way of blocking things out.

But these protective barriers, this theory continues, can be removed so that more knowledge enters, thus expanding the mind. Probably one way of removing them is by the intake of drugs. Or they are perhaps broken down in certain forms of mental illness. In these cases, the floodgates are opened and reality rushes in, often with horrendous and traumatic consequences. Or again, some people may be born with less restrictive filters; and these are the 'psychics' who are open to telepathy, clairvoyance and other parapsychological sources of information. Meditation is also a human and natural way of opening the filters, welcoming the inflow of reality, and expanding the mind. It is a gradual process, a daily practice, in which the filters or barriers are slowly lifted to allow an almost imperceptible inflow of greater reality into the intuitive consciousness—though this unhurried process may, at times, give way to a sudden collapse of barriers that causes massive enlightenment or mystical experience. In all this, meditation is safer than drugs because the meditator, if properly instructed and guided, can integrate the new knowledge and preserve his equilibrium.

The Paiute shamans came to these very rocks where I now sit to induce visions that would help them break through into the unseen world, to commune with the spirits on behalf of their tribe. Because of their experiences, they became powerful leaders, and, in some cases, sexual predators. While they enjoyed a position at the center of tribal life, they lived in constant fear of losing their power as a result of forgetting their visions.

Is the institution of the Christian clergy a form of shamanism? I have found that my validation as pastor to my congregation comes not from university degrees or my professional standing within the Diocese of Los Angeles. Rather, I have found that it is through regular meditation, focusing on passages of the scriptures, and regular retreats into the desert to be with God, that my parishioners have found in me a renewed spiritual guide who can inspire, coach and encourage a deepening relationship with God. Out of my weakness and brokenness, not personal power, I have found my authentic path of discipleship with Jesus.

And, as with the shamans who kept returning to these rocks, true spiritual power has to be carefully managed, maintained, at least as much from within the self as by the institutions outside. Otherwise the power corrupts.

Clergy sexual misconduct is a grievous example of such corruption. Pastors and priests are privileged to be with people at their most vulnerable. But if clergy do not have a regular practice of self-reflection, nor avail themselves of a spiritual director or therapist, the power that they embody can cause them to act towards vulnerable people in hurtful, even predatory ways.

Churches are developing systems of education, psychological testing during seminary training, and 'no-tolerance' policies, to prevent sexual misconduct of the clergy. That is the institutional response. The personal response is also an essential part of the 'wellness' that the Church now actively fosters. It includes a regular prayer life, membership in a colleague support group, and official witness to the importance of the retreat where the individual can rest in God's love.

I hope that these notes on the Spirit in the Desert will help and encourage especially my sisters and brothers who serve the Church to find soul-health here in the wildness of the Owens Valley. Don't let your spiritual life become an empty page, as my spiritual life once was.

Hiking in the Owens Valley. Photograph: Janice Karelius, 1995

Extra Directions to the Volcanic Tablelands Petroglyphs.

Driving north on Highway 395 through Bishop, look for signs to Highway 6 at the 'Y' at the north end of the town. Highway 6 will continue north and then east toward Laws. At Laws, the site of a terrific railroad museum, Highway 6 will continue north, eventually over Montgomery Pass into Nevada.

About 15 miles north of Laws on Highway 6, look for Childago Canyon Road (mile-marker 19). Take the road to the left toward the hill westward. You will pass a large hay barn on your left. The road will travel the shoulder of the hill, heading northwest. Be very vigilant for free-range cattle on this road. The road will come to an 'H' intersection. Childago Canyon Road will go right and north. A dirt road will connect to Fish Slough Road. Look carefully at this intersection. Small BLM warning signs will appear and you can see places where cars have parked. You have arrived at the Red Canyon Petroglyph Site.

After you have visited this site, you may continue south on Fish Slough Road for about 6 miles and you will come to the Childago Canyon Petroglyphs. Prominent among a large pile of boulders is Newspaper Rock, crowded with rock drawings.

Retracing your journey back to Highway 6, turn right, heading back toward Bishop. In about 2.2 miles you will see a dirt road heading in a southwest direction. Take this road about 0.9 miles to the Chalfant Petroglyph Site. This is a large area of rock carvings. Here I found some circle drawings of more than five feet in diameter.

POSTLUDE

I began this book in 1997. My time with the Spirit in the desert has made three great differences in my life.

First, Erik's health has become more stable. Today he is a handsome twenty-five year old, with a mental age of four or five. He needs constant supervision and continues to sleep in a bed next to me at night. For many years he attended an excellent special education program with the Orange County Department of Education. My wife, Jan, and I were anxious when he turned twenty-two because after that there were few other programs available to him. But our social worker guided us to a non-profit program which provides supervision for the developmentally disabled with appropriate work and recreational opportunities.

The Jewish mystic Martin Buber wrote that when we are looking for God in difficult times, "people are God's language." Look for the people who come into your life at critical moments. God sent us a wonderful man in Bill Remington. Bill has two children of his own and has a big heart for Erik. Each weekday, Bill comes to our home and takes Erik and another young man out into the community. They go for long walks, do some volunteer work, such as putting away videos in the Laguna Beach Library, have lunch, and sometimes go swimming. Erik comes home every day tired, but happy. He continues to live in the present moment, with no fears or anxieties, loves music from the 1950s-60s, and is basically content. He has been surrounded by love and prayer his entire life.

THE SPIRIT IN THE DESERT

The remarkable stability of his health the past few years is the result of a new microsurgery. Erik had a Vegus Nerve Stimulator implanted in 2000 at Children's Hospital of Orange County by Dr. Michael Mahonan, M.D. The implant is similar to a pacemaker, being located under the skin of his upper left breast. A wire runs from the implant up the left side of his neck to the vegus nerve. It emits an electrical pulse that stimulates the vegus nerve and the brain which seems to scramble the seizures. A paddle connected to a notebook computer can adjust the frequency and bandwidth.

For two years following the surgery we did not notice a change. Then, dramtically, during the third year Erik went from having at least sixty full tonic-clonic seizures per month to about ten. He can now go three or four days without a seizure, but he can still have one at any time. Usually they happen during sleep. He can still go into *status epilepticus,* but Valium stops this. As a result of the VNS implant, Erik's medications have been cut by about sixty percent. He no longer has to take Dylantin which kept him alive but caused terrible damage to his gums and stomach. He is more alert and I think he is happier. He laughs with a deep gusto.

We did not think Erik would live this long. Now we found ourselves planning for his care as we got on in years. We added to our home, creating a space where our daughter Katie can have her own home and be able to stay in Orange County. And as Katie follows her own dreams she has the option of living close to us and helping care for Erik. He is especially fond of his sister.

My time in the desert has allowed me to step back from the day-to-day care and concern for Erik. When I walk in the Owens Valley, I can look back at all the hard times and remember how God speaks to us in the helping presence of many persons, and I am thankful.

Second, Jan has achieved her dream of becoming a Family Nurse Practitioner. During Erik's hospitalizations, as we watched in his room, Jan would study for her exams or write her MSN thesis. Some days it seemed to her that the efforts were futile, because life for Erik was fragile and our own lives flip-flopped from hour to hour. I would encourage her to take one more step, one more class. Finally, after almost three decades as an Emergency Room R.N. and professor of nursing at Saddleback College, Mission Viejo, she would be the first nurse practitioner on the medical staff at South Coast Medical Center. As I walk in the desert I am grateful to have Jan in my life and as a partner in caring for Erik.

Third, I have decided to stay at Messiah Parish until I retire. I prayed to God for the grace to stay in Santa Ana and not to go off to 'bigger and better' projects. My time with the Spirit in the desert made the difference. Walking in the sandswept open space, in a landscape as big as God's heart, my heart and soul quieted. The beauty and majesty of creation spilling out before me was so wonderful to behold that it could hurt. That inner voice that criticizes everyone, making me feel like I am unappreciated and unloved, became silent. Here with the Spirit in the desert, I come again to a presence that is love. My heart fills with thanksgiving and gratitude for all of God's goodness, for the privilege of being a priest, and for surviving thirty-seven years of ministry, still with faith and passion for the difficult work of ministry in the city.

As a result of my decision to remain in Santa Ana, our parish, in partnership with other religious communities, has established two life-changing ministries.

The Noah Project was founded in 1996 as a response to the fifty-percent dropout-rate of eighth-graders in our neighborhood. Luan Mendel and Glenn Howard founded the first after-school academic learning centers at our parish and at St. Joseph's Roman Catholic School five blocks east. Since that time, the Noah Project has grown into an organization called Think Together. Today two hundred elementary and teen learning centers are active in Orange and Los Angeles Counties, and Think Together has become one of the premier learning centers in America. The tutoring program at our parish is now called the Noah Teen Center. We offer innovative programs in math tutoring and creative writing.

In 1999 a vacant medical building across the street from my church went on the real estate market. With two Sisters of St. Joseph, Sister Marianna Gemmet and Sister Eileen McNerney, I contemplated what kind of ministry could be based there that would serve our neighborhood. A remarkable collaborative emerged and Hands Together—a Center for Children opened on Valentine's Day 2000. The program now provides high quality early childhood education, reading readiness, health assessments, including speech, hearing, vision, dental and pediatric exams, to the poorest children living in Santa Ana, with parenting and nutrition classes for their parents. The center serves 92 children, age six weeks to five years, with a waiting list of 700 prequalified children. In 2001 HUD named Hands Together as an outstanding national example of 'projects that work.' During his visit to Santa Ana in September 2003, President George W. Bush expressed his personal thanks to me for our congregation's work with children and youth.

THE SPIRIT IN THE DESERT

As you and I visit the sacred sites of Owens Valley, we should enter with openness to the Spirit's touch and inspiration in this wild place. In this book I have not attempted to create a travel narrative nor to share a collection of 'peak experiences.' That is done better elsewhere. Instead, I have simply tried to convey that with a straightforward trust in God's wonders: from the indominatable spirit of Manzanar to the mysterious Power of a Paiute pine-nut harvest, there is a richness which anyone can own. We come into the desert, this powerful space to walk beneath the scrutinizing light of God's loving presence. We come for inspiration and course correction in our pilgrimage, for solace and for strength, and for pardon and renewal. You and I cannot be the same persons after walking in the sacred sites of the Owens Valley.

Books and Articles Mentioned in the Text

Abbey, Edward. *The Best of Edward Abbey.* San Francisco: Sierra Club Books, 1984.

Barry, William. *Who Do You Say I Am? Meeting the Historical Jesus in Prayer.* Notre Dame, Indiana: Ave Maria Press, 1996.

Cooper, Ellen. *How It Was: Some Memories by Early Settlers of the Indian Wells Valley and Vicinity.* Ridgecrest, California: Historical Society of the Upper Mojave Desert, 1994.

Delacourt, Michael. *The Prehistory of the Owens Valley.* Caltrans., CSU Sacramento, 2000.

Endo, Shusaku. *A Life of Jesus.* Mahwah, New Jersey: Paulist Press, 1978.

Foster, Lynne. *Adventuring in the California Desert.* San Francisco: Sierra Club Travel Guide, 1997.

Gilreath, Amy. *Prehistoric Use of the Coso Volcanic Field (volume 56).* Berkeley, California: University of California Berkeley Archaeological Research Facility, 1997.

Gomes, Peter. Sermons: *Biblical Wisdom for Daily Living.* Boston: William Morrow, 1998.

Grey, Zane. *Wanderer of the Wasteland.* New York: Grosset and Dunlap, 1923.

Johnston, William. *Silent Music: The Science of Meditation.* New York: Fordham University Press, 1997.

Lanner, Ronald. *The Piñon Pine: A Natural and Cultural History.* Reno, Nevada: University of Nevada Press, 1981.

Leech, Kenneth. *True God.* London: Sheldon Press, 1985.

McCarthy, Thomas. The Ultimate Sanctum. *America,* April 9, 2001.

Merton, Thomas. *Thoughts in Solitude.* New York: Farrar, Straus & Giroux, 1958.

———— *New Seeds of Contemplation.* New York: New Directions Publishing, 1978.

Moses, John. *The Desert: an Anthology for Lent.* Harrisburg, Pennsylvania: Morehouse Publishing, 1997.

Otto, Rudolf. *The Idea of the Holy.* New York: Oxford University Press, 1958.

Pisarowicz, James. *Proceedings of the Third Death Valley Conference on History and Prehistory.* Death Valley, California: Death Valley Natural History Association, 1992.

———— *Proceedings of the Fourth Death Valley Conference on History and Prehistory.* Death Valley, California: Death Valley Natural History Association, 1994.

Shaw, Tom. *Meditations for the Diocese of Los Angeles Clergy Conference.* Long Beach, California: Episcopal Diocese of Los Angeles, 1996.

Sheldrake, Philip. *Living Between Worlds: Place and Journey in Celtic Spirituality.* Boston: Cowley Publications, 1990.

Steinmetz, Paul (Ed.) *Meditations with Native Americans—Lakota Spirituality.* Santa Fe, New Mexico: Bear & Co., 1984.

Whitley, David. *A Guide to Rock Sites: Southern California and Southern Nevada.* Missoula, Montana: Mountain Press, 1996.

Wills, Garry. *John Wayne's America: the Politics of Celebrity.* New York: Simon & Schuster, 1997.

Wuerthner, George. *California's Wilderness Areas: the Complete Guide.* Englewood, Colorado: Westcliffe Publishers, 1997.

FURTHER READING

Austin, Mary. *The Basket Woman: A Book of Indian Tales.* Reno: University of Nevada Press, 1904.

Brooks, Joan. *The Desert Padre: the Life and Writings of Father John J. Crowley, 1891–1940.* Buena Vista, Colorado: the Mesquite Press, 1997.

Chalfant, W. A. *The Story of Inyo.* Bishop, CA: Chalfant Press, 1933.

Clark, Lewis and Virginia. *High Mountains and Deep Valleys: the Gold Bonanza Days.* San Luis Obispo: Western Trails Publications, 1987.

Dunne, Tad. *Spiritual Exercises for Today: A Contemporary Presentation of the Classic Spiritual Exercises of Ignatius Loyola.* San Francisco: Harper San Francisco, 1991.

Ewan, Rebecca Fish. *A Land Between: Owens Valley, California.* Baltimore: Johns Hopkins University Press, 2000.

Halfpenny, James. *A Field Guide to Mammal Tracking in North America.* Boulder, Colorado: Johnson Printing Company, 1986

Hogue, Lawrence. *All the Wild and Lonely Places: Journeys in a Desert Landscape.* Washington, DC: Island Press, 2000.

Holland, Dave. *On Location in Lone Pine.* Granada Hills, CA: The Holland House, 1990.

Jaeger, Edmund C. *The California Deserts.* Stanford: Stanford University Press, 1965.

Lane, Belden C. *The Solace of Fierce Landscapes: Exploring Desert and Mountain Spirituality.* New York: Oxford University Press, 1998.

Lanning, Edward F. *Archaeology of the Rose Spring Site, INY-373.* Berkeley: University of California Press, 1963.

Olson, Wilma R. *Olancha Remembered.* Sacramento, W. R. Olson, 1997.

Putnam, Jeff, and Smith, Genny. *Deepest Valley: Guide to Owens Valley, It's Roadsides and Mountain Trails.* Mammoth Lakes, CA: Genny Smith Books, 1995.

Rolheiser, Ronald. *The Holy Longing: The Search for a Christian Spirituality.* New York: Doubleday, 1999.

Smith, Genny (Ed.) *Sierra East: Edge of the Great Basin.* Berkeley: University of California Press, 2000.

Steward, Julian H. *Ethnography of the Owens Valley Paiute.* Berkeley: University of California Press, 1933.

Whitley, David. *A Guide to Rock Sites: Southern California and Southern Nevada.* Missoula, Montana: Mountain Press, 1996.

Appendix One: Other Resources and Websites

Center for Spiritual Development
480 S. Batavia
Orange, CA 92868.
(714) 744-3175
A ministry of the Sisters of Saint Joseph of Orange. Excellent resource for finding a spiritual director. They also have a calendar of ecumenical retreats and workshops. Overnight retreat space available. www.thecsd.org

Eastern California Museum
155 North Grant Street, PO Box 206
Independence CA 93526
(760) 878-0364
Independence is located about 15 minutes drive north of Lone Pine. The museum is open daily (except Tuesday) 10am to 4pm. Here you will find an extensive collection of Owens Valley history, including Owens Valley Paiute and the Manzanar Camp, a research library, and a bookstore. Annual membership includes an excellent newsletter.

Owens Valley Paiute Shoshone Cultural Center
2301 West Line Street,
Bishop, CA 93514
(760) 873-4478
The museum offers excellent informative displays featuring the history of the Owens Valley tribes.

Maturango Museum
100 E. Las Flores Ave.
Ridgecrest, CA 93555
(619) 375-6900.

Open 10am to 5pm, Wednesday through Sunday. This museum of the Northern Mojave Desert has extensive exhibits, a bookstore, and leads field trips to mining towns and geological sites. Each spring and fall, trips are conducted to the Petroglyph Canyon Historical Monument at the Naval Air Weapons Stations, China Lake. These visits provide access to the finest petroglyphs in the United States. The Historical Society has an excellent newsletter and calendar of lectures.

Beverly and Jim Rogers Museum of Lone Pine Film History.
Highway 395
Lone Pine, CA
(760) 876-9103
www.lonepinefilmhistory.org.
Excellent display of memorabilia from the many Western films made in the Lone Pine area, including an excellent short film to orient you to the location of these films.

Manzanar National Historic Site.
Located nine miles north of Lone Pine, on Highway 395.
(760) 868-2194
www.nps.gov/manz

**

http://anglicansonline.org
An excellent resource on everything about the Episcopal Church and the worldwide Anglican Communion.

http://www.coyotepress.com
The Coyote Press prints copies of important anthropological and archaeological research on Native Americans. Good resource for information on Northern Paiutes and Owen Valley Paiutes.

www.desertusa.com
A guide to the peoples and cultures of the Southwest.

www.messiah-santaana.org

Comprehensive resource for ministries, sermons and programs from the Episcopal Church of the Messiah, Santa Ana, CA.

www.395.com

A wealth of information about the Owens Valley and all of the communities along Highway 395. Includes up-to-date information about climbing Mount Whitney.

www.owensvalleyhistory.com

Terrific resource for history and culture of the Owens Valley, including information about the original 'Desert Padre,' Father Crowley.

www.dowvillamotel.com

Historic hotel in Lone Pine, where many Western film stars have stayed.

www.canyonrecords.com

Traditional songs from pinenut festival—use search tool for Judy Trejo, Tuhva Tzi Buina (Pinenut Blessing Song), Circle Dance Songs, and Arlie Neskahi, Welcoming Song

Appendix Two: An Example of a Sermon Following a Desert Pilgrimage. June 1997

I am standing within a sand dune on the northern edge of Owens Lake, near the High Sierra. Buffeted by constant winds, the dunes shift and move. The anchors for the dunes are some four-foot high bushes, here and there.

I walk over to a dune bush and bend to my knees. The bush is covered with seedpods. At the base of the plant is a depression filled with old seeds. I gather a handful—hundreds of little seeds that have not germinated. Only a few do, in these dry sand dunes on the edge of a salty lake. I lift the handful of seeds and toss them into the wind. They take off into the far distance.

One tiny seed is stuck to the sweat on my palm. I compare this tiny little seed with the bulk of the mother plant, and of course I remember today's parable of the mustard seed. I see the contrast between this little seed, and the large green bush anchored in the dune, which is a habitat to a vast desert ecosystem.

There is more to this parable.

Jesus chose a humble, wild plant to describe the Kingdom of God. In our gospel reading for this morning, we imagine Jesus with a mustard seed sticking to the sweat of his palms. Jesus holds up his hands so we see the tiny seed, a sign of the secrets about the Kingdom in our very midst. We do not control the results of this Kingdom. What matters is that we are available to be grown by the Holy Spirit. What matters is that you and I are present to God.

Once again, Jesus shakes up our culturally-conditioned reality. Small is large. A tiny infant born in a cave becomes Savior of the World. Jesus identifies a little child as the model disciple. Very little food can feed five thousand people.

In his book, *The Holy Longing,* Ron Rolheiser shares:

When we open to the wonder of the small, in the hands of God, we see the power of small working amongst us.

A small gesture makes a large impression.

A small phrase (I do, I love you), makes a lasting impact.

A small gift, can express wondrous love.

A small idea can launch a computer industry and change the world.

God plants the Word within us. In the ripening of time and with grace, our soul grows. We are drawn to the way Jesus lives with people.

And we plant seeds of the Word around us. In *Agape* love we do and act and give without demanding response.

And God nurtures the seeds we plant.

Can you sense the presence of the Word planted within you?

Do you see yourself planting seeds with God?

Do you sense a sacred pulse, a movement in your life, that seems to connect the pieces together, and sometimes bubbles up as hope and joy and peace and love for you at the most surprising times?

I am often surprised how seeds of grace, which take root in a receptive, hospitable soil, grow into bushes that become spiritual ecosystems for others.

I remember, about thirteen years ago when Sister Beth Burns started a summer dance company, about this time in June, when schools let out. A dance group for neighborhood girls in our choir room. Little by little, in an environment of prayer, nurturing self-esteem and discipline, and motherly care, God grew the St. Joseph Ballet Company into a wonderful plant.

I remember Al Doby approaching the church to host the after school Pride Program. And with the attention of Glenn and Joyce Howard, and Luan Mendel and others of you, the seed was received and has taken root into the Noah Teen Center that will be launched here at Messiah this September.

In both cases, I suppose someone could have done a detailed feasibility study, researched location, and identified Messiah as a potential location for programs in the inner city. But the wonder and joy, for those who have worked in the trenches of building these programs, is things never turn out the way you plan.

There has been more going on here than human effort.

Where mission and service, hospitality, love and acceptance are modeled, this is good soil to grow the Kingdom. In the most unlikely places. And the soil of this old church seems to be especially receptive.

Do you sense something growing in you? Do you sense movement, that you are being drawn into some action, some involvement, in the name of Jesus. But you are not sure what it is?

I remember some years ago when Barbara Henderson told me she was going to retire as a manager of a branch of the Auto Club of Southern California. She said she was sensing a call to ministry in Spanish. She didn't speak Spanish. In time Barbara has become an important leader with the Comite and OCCCCO.

We do not control the results of the Kingdom. What matters is our availability to being grown by the Holy Spirit.

It means being present to God and being open to receiving the kingdom.

I read books on leadership, vision casting, and planning.

Where is the map to help me grow spiritually and grow the church?

The map is still within me and within you.

The map is the mystical connection you and I have with God.

Our attentive presence and availability to God.

Here, in the heart of the seeker of God, small is always great.

Thanks be to God.

ABOUT THE AUTHOR

Photograph: Ann Avery Andres, Swansea Wells Fargo Station

Father Brad Karelius, an Episcopal priest in the Diocese of Los Angeles, has been Rector of Messiah Parish, Santa Ana, California, since 1981. He has also been part-time professor of philosophy and world religions at Saddleback College in Mission Viejo since 1973. He is a member of the Nevada Archaeological Society, the American Philosophical Association and the California Cattlemen's Association. He is married and has two children.

Made in the USA
Columbia, SC
12 June 2021